SUNDAY OUT OF NOWHERE

NEW AND SELECTED POEMS

SUNDAY OUT OF NOWHERE

NEW AND SELECTED POEMS

BRIAN SWANN

The Sheep Meadow Press
Rhinebeck, New York

Designed and typeset by Sheep Meadow Press
Distributed by The University Press of New England

Cover Image: photograph: Tetsuo Abe, Matisse's studio, Hôtel Régina, Nice

Library of Congress Cataloging-in-Publication Data

Names: Swann, Brian, author.
Title: Sunday out of nowhere : new and selected poems / Brian Swann.
Description: Rhinebeck, New York : The Sheep Meadow Press, 2018.
Identifiers: LCCN 2018017013 | ISBN 9781937679804 (pbk.)
Classification: LCC PS3569.W256 A6 2018 | DDC 811/.54--dc23
LC record available at https://lccn.loc.gov/2018017013

All inquiries and permission requests should be addressed to the publisher:

Sheep Meadow Press
PO Box 84
Rhinebeck, NY 12514

PRESCRIPT

These are the seven collections I have drawn from:

LIVING TIME,
(winner, Quarterly Review of Literature Contemporary Poetry Series, 1978)

THE MIDDLE OF THE JOURNEY,
(winner, University of Alabama Press Poetry Series, 1982)

AUTUMN ROAD,
(winner, The Ohio State University Press/ *The Journal* Award in Poetry,
Ohio State University Press, 2005)

SNOW HOUSE,
(winner, Lena-Miles Wever Todd Poetry Series, Pleiades Press/LSU Press, 2006)

IN LATE LIGHT,
(Johns Hopkins University Press, 2013)

ST. FRANCIS AND THE FLIES,
(winner, Autumn House Poetry Prize, Autumn House Press, 2015)

 COMPANIONS, ANALOGIES,
(Sheep Meadow Press, 2016)

An earlier version of "Poetry and Birds" appeared in *Plume Poetry.*

In the 'New Poems' section, these are the credits:

Georgia Review: "The Fens," "1630s"
Hudson Review: "A Word," "The Wait," "The Diagnosis"
Michigan Quarterly Review: "Spring Clean"
Raritan: "Cardiac," "Wild Apples"
Salmagundi: "Elegiac," "Theseus' Ship," "The Eternal Return"
Southern Review: "An Unfinished Nude"
The Plume Anthology of Poetry, 5: "Cozumel"
The Plume Anthology of Poetry, 6: "Journal, or Story Without Words"

    I have not included poems from three of my early books, *The Whale's Scars* (New Rivers Press, 1974), *Roots* (New Rivers Press, 1978), and *Paradigms of Fire* (Corycian Press, 1980). They were apprentice work, *The Whale's Scars* learning by translating (from Anglo-Saxon, Old Norse and the Spanish of Homero Aridjis), while *Roots* worked with imitation and adaptation from, for example, Ferenc Juhasz's "The Boy Turned into a Stag Cries at the Gate of Dreams." This collection also experimented with dialect in "Northern Garland," a Basil Bunting inspired long poem using my native Northumbrian. *Paradigms of Fire* was an excursus into surrealism. I have also omitted work from *Song of the Sky: Versions of Native American Song-Poems* (University of Massachusetts Press, 1985/ 1993) and *Wearing the Morning Star: Native American Song-Poems* (Random House, 1996), since they are not stand-alone poems but "song-poems" based on translations; they are "versions" that have passed through mediations and filters, accompanied by linguistic and anthropological materials.

ACKNOWLEDGEMENTS

The New Yorker, American Scholar, Sewanee Review, Yale Review, Chicago Review, Paris Review, Partisan Review, New Republic, Harvard Review, Poetry, Harper's, Hopkins Review, Bennington Review, Canto, Mid-American Review, Notre Dame Review, Poetry Northwest, Prairie Schooner, Boulevard, The Iowa Review, Michigan Quarterly Review, New England Review, Poet Lore, Raritan, The Southern Review, New Letters, Salmagundi, Stand (GB), Warwick Review (GB), Agni, American Literary Review, Ploughshares, Cincinnati Review, Gettysburg Review, Hudson Review, Parnassus, Poetry East, Western Humanities Review, Miramar Poetry Journal, Plume Poetry, The Plume Anthology of Poetry, Ploughshares, The North American Review, Chicago Review, Georgia Review, Massachusetts Review, Missouri Review, Poetry Daily.

CONTENTS

from *ST. FRANCIS AND THE FLIES*

from COMPANIONS, ANALOGIES

from LIVING TIME

PIAZZA S. EGIDIO, 9

Signor Clementi is deaf and therefore whispers.
He has to tell me that the strange-looking box
is a fireplace for burning wood. Wood–
he points to a chair leg. I know what wood is.
He tells me where the garbage goes,
that the bell always chimes on the hour,
that a two-pronged plug won't go
into a three-pronged hole, that electricity is
very expensive and takes me down to read
the meters, that the current's weak and therefore
not to use the oven with the broiler on.
He tells me that his dog is not *cattivo*,
or won't be once he gets to know me,
but I don't think of dogs as I run down
to ask him to rescue me, dragging him from dinner,
because all the lights are out.
He pushes the other end of something
I thought I'd broken when I smashed into it
with the dresser I was moving, and the lights come up.

I lie down, and fall between two beds. I thought
it was a double bed. I'd asked for a double bed.
I lie listening to the new apartment, its creaks,
the noises my neighbors make, the voices
from the alleyway, someone revving up a bike,
and the bell I'm beginning to tolerate.
Then, to pull it all together, go out,
cross the Ponte Sisto, and on the corner
buy a bunch of mimosa and
one red rose, the same one I bought
which you kept in a wine bottle till the water
dried and the rose was dust.

And now they stand on top of the dresser,
waiting for me to finish with the table
so their scent can creep lower, take over,
creep into every corner, into the fireplace
and round the radiator that squirted my leg
when I turned what I thought was the on-valve.
And it will lie in wait for you, as you walk
through the strange door, wondering what is to be
your home, you who are now
six hours back, but soon to catch up
and run our times together.

RAPUNZEL

The baroque chapel has two putti who pull
aside a stone curtain which now leads
into a trattoria.
Next door a basket hangs by a cord
from an open window. On this first hot
March day, a girl looms from the back
to block the window like a gray boulder.
She places her transistor on the sill and
delicately tunes it to screaming pitch,
till she jams even the canaries
and motorbikes. She rests her forearms
beside the music and gazes down
into the lane. The basket sways just below her,
empty. "Innamorato sempre di più,"
the battery voice soars. Her eyes rest
on the slowly swaying basket,
which each morning she lowers and
pulls up again, full of bread, and cheese,
and a magazine.

STORM

For Patrick and Ursula Creagh

I have put in a window, painted all round
white, while the rain pocked the cement
and rinsed the whitewash before it could dry.
Rain continues dripping down the chimney
onto the juniper that was smoking the ham,
hissing it out. Rain goes on, off, on, off.
Lightning pokes in and out like a needle.
I hear the cry of the cock pheasant
in the oat-field; go to tie up vines, but
turn back. The dog, scavenging all day,
lies first on one chair, then the sofa, then
on each bed, keeping a watery eye on me.
Every time I move, he gets up. When I turn
back, he turns back too. The goat under
the window has wound herself round her peg
and bleats to be taken in. I unravel her,
and she stands stinking in the fireplace,
thinking it's winter.
        I pick up a bleary color
photo of a woman with flowers in her hair,
holding a basket of flowers, throwing blossoms
at a light in the courtyard window.
        In the old days,
these peasant houses had windows only
in the darkest and lowest parts. The peasants
had enough of fine views as they worked
the wiry fields. A house was to sleep in,
nothing to see in the powerful dark which
rises over the ridge above the house, throwing
black flowers at the window.

HIDING

Arbitrarily, I have chosen a window:
gorse, a burnt ridge, three power lines
cutting across, a farmhouse.
Beyond the dust this side and the rain
that, great flimsy bellies of cobwebs.

A child's voice blurs at the other end
of the house, interrupted by the click
of beetles in the beams and the scent
of broom in brass pitchers. Hams hang
aging, which is to say, slowly going rotten.

A child's voice, closer, asks where I am.
I am not here. I am in hiding,
as on the first night, years ago,
before she was born, slipping out
into fields to watch fireflies like
sulfurous planets pulse over the barely
broken land, under a sky full of stars,
imitating them. And thinking: there are
other fields and houses beyond this,
in hiding. And beyond that, still more,
otherwise great gaps would open in the sky,
Beyond that, however, they are not
hiding. They are not unknown.
But they are not known.

BURNING

The sun is climbing the door
like a wind.
It brings glass into play
on a whole hillside caught in its own absoluteness,
in the gleam of itself that renders
detail as circumstance.
It is absorbed into the door-frame,
into the cracked floor,
into the rooms piled on one another
like shrunken apricots.

They have burned the fields in black strips.
The forest hill has been fired by hunters
and is reflected in the sky.
No one has woken yet as
a bed creaks and goes quiet.

The charcoal in the grate is clicking still.
In the cantina
wine is exploding its darkness.
Each chair and table has the crust of its shape upon it.

The farmer
is dreaming of the snake by the spring,
the crab he found in the wet grass of the vineyard,
boulders in the roots of uptorn olives,
the slant glances of his young wife.

THE OCTOPUS

The waves come in through the shutters,
water whipped to white, fish-smelling,
clean as a fish-scale, calling
to the shell in her ear, the plasma that is thick
salt-water, the heart that is
an octopus, its ink silhouette
pounded into wharf concrete,
the soggy thump still heard
as the fisherman picks it up
and hurls it down again,
dips it in a bucket,
beats again, then
kneads it one-handed, firm
and gentle as a masseur,
in the body's white suds.
He cuts and hangs the flesh
on a line, like a hat
in shreds, flesh that was
subtle, shy, under
its own rock, its long arms
prying and attaching.

BIG FRIDAY

"It is too easy and pagan to use everything
as metaphor for the self, the self is
not just what it sees. And to haunt things
looking for what we are makes it all
a parlor game."
          The words of the little priest
drift away with the little boat
that brought me across where rocks are
honeycombed like minute hermit cells.
I sit in the deserted monastery which someone
is clearly tending, since the goat head
on the wall does not seem out of place.
I set out for my roofless stone hut
by the three bent pines. A kid's call
comes downwind like a mosquito's whine.
I walk beside a wheatfield, blue stalks,
green heads, by a field fresh broken
for vines, leaves soft enough to eat.
A stem lies snapped, perhaps a stray goat foot.
Sap has rushed out and continues to flow,
water sucked up from the heart of stones.
Two ritual bird-dancers in gray and black
give themselves away by too vivid flight
from a stone wall. I stand outside the hut.
Distant goat-bells like breaking glass
arrive at the same time as the distant church
across the water with its toll
for Christ dead. Above my head
the crazy half-moon pupil of the billy-goat,
wary at my intrusion.
The bells stop, wait in silence
for the boulder pushed aside, the call of
"Christ is risen."
It is a good day for Christ to rise.

ISTANBUL

I wonder why I've returned to this place
that behaves as if a city is cinder-blocks and planks,

sheepskins nailed to the sides of houses,
forgotten, going rank. Where the people

live in coal smoke and kids swim in wide
slicks of garbage after work, and I remember when

I was a boy, seeing older kids like a foreign race,
black with pit or shipyard, drifting

through coal smoke, crumbling streets,
and thinking: *that* is how things are,

that's real life, the sizing-up of a
sharp look, the thick gob of spit,

the crushed stub of a cigarette, the breath
that takes in foul air like a joke.

LIVING TIME

In a rush against time I press my back
to the window, holding the page mirror-flat
against a world where the sun has dropped
behind Istinye. Its light, now paper-thin,
drifts around looking for someplace
to settle. I look out of the side-windows.
Colors are agonistic: laburnum yellow,
acacia's white, lilac's deliberate purple.
I try to catch and hold this last light
on the page, while the room sours
primitively. The nightingale, who has sung
all day in the same cypress almost lost
in looser sounds, bubbles up in a clear
fall of water. I have trimmed the filthy
wick, scrounged from the bottom of drawers
three stubs of candle. I hold off to the last,
hoping to finish what there is to say
before the dark of my hand on the paper
deadens the point, and what is to be said
gets lost in the cold mist gathering
in valleys that drop steep
to the slippery waters of the Bosphorus,
its few lights sliding dirty yellow,
up and down, across, along.

from THE MIDDLE OF THE JOURNEY

RED UMBRELLA

You go along. Your father dies. You
walk into the kitchen one morning. It
is bright. Your father is there. Your
mother is there. You smile at your
mother. Your mother is radiance. You
wake with your face and pillow wet.
Your hands hurt with climbing a fence
to the roof. From there you can see
all along the gardens. Fruit trees,
asparagus on raised beds. Birds
fly up to you. The fence high as
a house bends. You are on your
hands and knees grubbing in the soil.
You go along. Your father is dead.
Someone who shares a shelter
from the rain with you says:
I was once in the China Sea.
There was a typhoon. The rain
came in silver sheets. Each wave
brought its own curtain of rain.
The boats were dragging their
anchors. We were all on deck in
life jackets. I was young so I
had no thoughts of death. You
say, it'll let up in ten minutes.
Water slicked with oil
runs in gutters like rope. He
jumps into the storm, sticking
a red umbrella out at it.
The sun gives a gray glow. You
watch the birds. You
go along.

REFLECTIONS

My grandmother and aunt took off
his oil-soaked clothes and
bathed him like a baby.
He didn't know where he was.
The Navy took him to King's Seat.
My mother said "Tall lovely Americans
sat playing with their fingers
in corridor after corridor."
Light drifted through high windows.
All you could hear was the
thin sound of breathing.
He sat in the corner, alone,
on a bench. He leaped away
from her. "I don't know you,"
he said. His mind has stopped,
the doctor whispered. Bring
your baby with you next time.
"You brought him round. We still
don't know what he's been through
all those years. You have to
make allowances. Have to."

The nose and its small broken veins
is whiter than my mother's powder
he used on it before venturing out.
It is sealed, the gray eye
with its cinder trapped
like an insect. In his rages
it was my awful focus.
My sister weeps. "Goodbye daddy.
I haven't called you that
for a long time." She wants to
kiss him, but is afraid. She
touches him instead. "He only said,
'Be kind. Be nice'."

Cold summer
air from the open window
above the casket thrums like wind
through the rigging of a ship.
The death mask is calm
after the explosion in the heart
that took him off where
depth-charge and torpedo
could not.

The morning I leave,
fen cirrus feathers over the sun.
A heron's curved prow sails over
the railroad sidings.
There's a reflection in the coach window.
The reflections go on as we pick up
speed. The reflections
go with us.

TURTLE FOUNTAIN

Light is sidetracked by open
french windows; swarms in

like bees swerving from
danced directions. Grandmother,

mother, aunt, sister, sit
in a row. I turn my grandmother's

face sideways against the light's
scattered pollen. My sister

sobs. I try to recall if
I'd told them the truth:

my father, old trickster,
he who had beaten his backside

black and blue for not keeping
guard while he slept, is

not dead. He has covered his
tracks, right down to the

plastic manikin he left in
the casket. "It's not him,"

my mother had said. She didn't know
how right she was. But I knew

the city he'd left for. I'd have
no trouble finding the small piazza

he'd chosen to live in. The one
with a fountain; four small boys

pushing turtles over the rim
back under the main fall of water.

BACK

This light is more than the light
that gets into the wind and makes it

depths and warm places, great pits
where the light comes and goes,

freeing itself from the river that
runs between charred prairie flowers

and wild vines when autumn fires have
swept the land black, and the only green

grows dully on islands. This light is
a child I wonder if I'll meet again

before it is too late. A child
who walks among skies of enormous blue

engined by the bursts of great stars.
He has taken a number of different

names. In his early world I wonder
if I'll find him sad, or smiling

inside a glass dome that settles over
everything as the sun fuses itself

into a quartz crystal, and birds,
as if carved from the branches they

perch on, retrace the same songs
again and again, each time somehow

different. There is a mirror the child
has hung in the woods. I would like

to walk toward it, right through
the depth, and keep going

forward, going, in fact, back.

LATE SPRING

Through the window I watch
the shadblow fall into
cold fragments. Petals of

White form a sky and confuse
the glass. Through a spider's
close chambers an invisible

Clue of wind ripples, darkening
the silk, leaving it light. I stand.
I cross the pasture. By

The pilings in the boatyard
fish turn with some
urgency. I watch one

Rise to a petal. I try
tracing things back to
real things. And turn

Round to where the house
seems to enclose its own shell,
and all the rooms echo

Each other. I hear my mother's
voice calling me by name,
It doesn't seem my name.

It doesn't seem like anybody's
name. The night before I had
dreamed of swimming. A hand

From below grasped my ankle
with small gentle fingers. Now
from behind the house I can smell

Smoke from the rakings, giving out.
Scents of light rain. On the
top of the maple's hanging few leaves

I can see the wing of a bird
brightening. The fire flares.
A shoulder of smoke collects

The storm gray and floats it off.
Everything is dissolved into
the derangement of late spring.

This morning I dug out
the streambed. A newt, commonest
of salamanders, startling

In adolescent pink, reached for
a rotten leaf with perfect fingers
of its left hand, missed, and

Corrected. Its eyes of damp soot
ducked under a stone, as new water
gathered over its head. It leaned

Against the fresh fall of water.
Rain is threatening again. I walk
back to the house, through the shadblow's

Confusion of seasons. I sit in my old seat,
while the window fills and clears.
Gray empty halls of the spider billow

And sag like old filmy lungs. The
small perfect hands had taken
my ankle. I swam for the shore, bent

Down, and pulled out a boy, white
as a frog belly, three years on
the bottom.

Wind filters through the web
stirring trains of images. The spider
from a far corner tugs on one

Of the brittle skeins, holds it for
a moment, then lets it fall.
The thread slackens, drops,

And drifts. Soon, along the wood's
damp places, newts in adult
lighted green will high-step through

Rotting leaves and fresh shoots.
They will head for rivers and
streams where they'll hang

As if suspended from a thread.

THE MIDDLE OF THE JOURNEY

1:
I lie in bed. Under my eyes, two
lines of snow like the canals

On Mars run down to a horizontal
lake mid-mountain. A town

Is seen over roofs of turning wheat,
blue-green. Red roofs, scarlet poppies,

In ditches. Valerian patches. More
red roofs like further fallen poppies,

Thrust and counter-thrust; parry
and surrender. It is not somewhere

I have been. Perhaps it is somewhere
I am going.

2:
The valley's long sound is
heightened by the silence. Hanging

In the silk-sound of the stream,
chickadees count invisible events

On the undersides of leaves. I
turn, and look back as if I could

Count each step that comes
straight at me, the grass lifting

Back up, paler. I stand where
the sky's axe-edge notches

The hill's top. If I could look at
my life now, it would be like finding

An old scratched daguerreotype of
someone I recognized but could not name.

3:
Daybreak. The comfortless wind
resists the comfort of sunrise.

Moths come too late, when the earth
has just turned. I mistake the moths

For snow, and the wind that clips
the curtains I mistake for

The wind that brings
bees and the metal scent

Of old lilacs. Fissures
in rock expand their darkness.

4:
Under my window a boy whistles
a tune so off-key and crude he must

Have made it up himself. The mind's
corners open. Snow begins to fall

Like the last light squeezed from leaves.
I lie in the dark, letting the season's

Final mosquito do with me what she wills.
I am floating just above the body,

My body dark, dreaming me, the
future, making itself up, linking

Itself to my discontinuity,
covering me like the embroidered

Bedspread my grandmother made
long before I was born.

LIKE BOATS

Who is this has come in
    and changed all the bedclothes,
folded them in neat piles in the closet
    so I don't know what
belongs where?

               Who
sent the cutlery into oblivion
    so I've had to eat everything
with my fingers?

               And who
sprayed milkweed with
    Krylon Acrylic Spray
and left the can with a wreath
    of dead daisies?

The rain knows no bounds.
    It has smothered horizons.
Mist sneaks into the house,
    and I burn the cheap bonded-sawdust
shed roof that collapsed
    in the first storm.

I collapse onto the sofa.
    Where are the insects?
The yellowjacket that stung me
    as I sat on the toilet
last time up; who almost
    killed me as I felt my heart
stop, then kick up again
    as I drove, dead, twenty miles
to the nearest clinic
    for allergy tests that
have set me back months?
    And where are my spiders

who eat my flies? And where
    are my flies?

            She's
exploded a bomb! I know
    its results. I'd done the same
two summers back, when the
    bank president's hippy
vegetarian daughter, who couldn't
    kill a living thing, had filled
the house with birds, who'd
    filled the house with fleas.
Who's never paid her rent.

I toss the orderly weeds
    into the back of the damp fire.
And dusty caterpillars of goldenrod
    she's perched in a precarious
glass vase over the fireplace
    drop, and shatter.

Where are the flies?
    Above the dash of the rain
I hear a small buzz.
    One dazed black fly
greets me like an old house
    from the corner of a chair.

In the night
    rain ate into my sleep.
I woke in my sleep
    and it stopped.
I woke
    and rain
had obliterated all distinction.

The glare of separation was in the room.

I push everything away from my life
    like boats.

JOY

Dawn arrived: a cat
with a bird in its mouth,
stepping dark and deliberate
toward my bed. But a bird
I'd never heard anywhere before
let alone in this city,
banged his little drum
down by the fountains
which had not yet started up
under my window.
In my head an Armenian nightingale
rose again like
smoke through water.

That day, all day, I hummed
a Hindi love song from some
Indian movie, all round town,
through the scent of the park's
new-cut grass and mayflower
in all its almost-sinister
sweetness of my childhood.
A squirrel came down his manicured tree
whiskers first, snuffled
through whatever feathery seeds
were left on the grass, and
threw himself into the air,
a whiplash, hooked salmon,
glove turned inside out.

from AUTUMN ROAD

HELIOGRAPHY

Losing I can accept,   a long process like mould.
That way I got to know this place   in another way,
like seeing the Pleiades   from the other side.
It could have been worse, I suppose.   I could
never have been here,   instead of having been flung
headlong into whatever it is,   light breaking over me
and fingertips reaching at me,   the old fat guide
picking me up. I'm your granny,   she said. And
your mammy, and your pappy,   god rest his whatever.
I will call you by your initial letter   and you will
live with me catty-corner.   You will eat your fingerprints
in silence, and everything   will resolve itself as if
a plot. She took me home   where keyholes made my eyes
lengthen and shrink until soon   it was time to leave.
They called it dead-man-time.   The prostitutes who had
taken me everywhere with them   spat the last seeds
into my mouth and sent me   on my way. They tasted
of seasons and the wild   gyrations of atoms. Conjecture,
introversion, wild surmise had   made up my world.
Now I needed new illusions.   Soon I was making up
my lives and the lives of others,   biographies to live
for themselves but in me   till I was full of inventories,
full of mirrors and ventriloquisms,   and a rusty angel
who faked his face but never   opened his mail, who
slept on the windowsill suspecting   rebuffs from every
angle, and who collided regularly   at take-off with
the same tree. But as for me   I grew a colon for eyes
and bells for ears. Shaken foil   was my trust, the Zodiac
my toy. So here I am, in a   parole of flowers, flapping
through libraries, outmoded,   outmatched, but not yet
old enough to be my own ghost.   So I place these ghosts
on paper, anonymous, ambiguous,   festive as a crowd
in an unnoticed world,   myself a character who will not
rehearse any more, determined still   to be someone similar to
who I am, but not me, keeping at it,   mistaking the sky for
something else, mistaking flashes   from my fingers for heliography!

PHYSICS

"This grand book of the universe...is written in the language of mathematics"
—Galileo

Under windows, boxes of polished brass and glass.
Inside, carefully balanced dust-proof scales &
below, in neat rows, brass weights like buttons,
arranged by size up & down the wooden floor.
Light caught inside bounced around unable to be measured,
at least by me though the promise was it could be if only
I could get the laws Mr.Bulman wrote on the board
day after day which everyone else got but
the only way I could was to copy their homework
which led to the deepest recesses of dark deceit.
So I sat in place, moving my head just a little at
a time to avoid detection & detention, up down all around
so everything flowed into everything else & the spectrum
split instead of staying still until the boxes
disappeared & everything in them into a gleam that turned
the sill to shining & everything on it & I knew
enough to know it all ended in my eyes (optics)
but from there, who knows, maybe it flew back out
to illuminate like headlights what had illuminated it
(guesswork) & this was how we knew the world
& maybe all the light that ever was had already been
in my eyes & out again, like the air everyone had breathed
since the start of time but which was still there,
so I swam in this element until the bell went
& we were dismissed into remaining light that had,
at one time or another, been us & we it, even though
now it was all mixed up with all sorts of other stuff,
and that was the way things were.

THE THIRD FACE

1:

I cry till I get my Scottish dancing pumps,
   soft as something I don't even know yet.
I wear them all the time. They are softer
   and more supple than skin. *Cissy.*
In my red hat and green jerkin I fold around
   myself. I endure the rot of school, debris
from all directions. Everybody talks.
I am trying to listen.

2:

It was all for the best. He meant well.
   I bet you're glad he's gone. He went,
but at the last moment a nurse's skirt
   almost changed his mind.
                              A drunk
is starting to weep. I am in another role now,
   something like a friend, dreaming
a dream before there were fathers, where
   I am in charge. I might be a character
in a story, someone making me up.

3:

All his mouths are merciless.
   I look forward to the day when,
all identity gone, I call my inventions
   just a child's cry, a walk in the dark.
It doesn't work. His great hands
   still grip. He still calls me *Cunt,*
Cissy, Crippen. Everyone except
   him has two faces.
One of mine is a murderer's.
   The other's a vulture.

THE POINT

My mother kneels at a pool
   giving off its own life like a fantastic book.
As evening comes down, she sees me in the dark,
   at the margin looking for that one lost touch,
a kind of paraphrase of touch, and a message,
   even fragment, that would open my hand,
even though I'm afraid of this primal vote
   of life and limb, a stranger to the bridge
and since we weren't a close family, nothing
   could go wrong. Still, to make sure I left almost
for ever, making my world clean as a seabird
   in the wind. But there she is connected
to herself in the pool, remembering
   in endlessness a concentrated someone who
went backwards to be more accessible
   to herself, and she turns and points at the real thing
which is not like the real thing at all,
   and starts to speak, but before she can finish
everything becomes extra and what had been
   like photography becomes a frame marked
Empty, and drowned faces flash like fish
   while I rustle and become a room to my own applause
dancing a Mr. Bones waving the leg of a calf.
   As light tilts, the whole sea sloshes over
and in the middle there she is still, my mother,
   kneeling at a pool, scrying, reciting in a foreign language
I can't even hear, but I think she's saying
   Let's work together. It was then I knew she wasn't
my mother. Old men don't have mothers.
   What would be the point?

RAIN OF THE WALDENSIANS

Late rain, humble, dedicated to the quiet virtues.
Rain falling on the Anatolian Bird Goddess
I bought in Turkey and placed in the arbor,
falling on the painting of St. Kevin I bought in Dublin
and placed on the porch, where he hatches
a nest of blackbirds in his hands.

From wood and hill the rain echoes like the bell
in which Modomnoc carried bees across the pure-colored sea
in a small boat sailing from the east. This rain
in plain dress cherishes the hidden seed: earnest and
humble craftsfolk about to stir their pale shoulders,
transform themselves and all around, turn inside-out
to form the coming reformation.

Objects all around me are silent and alone. Silence
is their speech and mine. From the blackness rain's
attracted to my light, its songs adagio, andante, crescendo,
dimuendo to the voices of things extinct. It runs along
whole fronts, wide curtains, whole centuries. It rains
my Hugeunot great-great-grandmother from Cevennes,
part of Pope Clement's "execrable race of the ancient Albigensians."
It rains those weavers, their caged birds and window boxes,
Friendly Societies and flower shows.

Next morning, an old lady watches drops slip off the ends
of mulberry leaves onto beans rising from underwater
to send out tendrils. Some she sees find nothing to grasp
and curl in on themselves. Some touch string, stick, and climb.
Others ascend themselves, or in mutual aid bridge synapses
one over another. The whole group is a nerve until they flower,
and then she'll say, "now they can breathe." She calls the cat.
He comes home late, splashing along the streambed like a small boy.

CONSUMED

In girum imus nocte et consumimur igni
(Latin palindrome)

like a tourist

W ho cannot leave while the town &

E nvirons are still lit up beyond midnight & multi-

C olored bunting hangs out as if

I t is always like that, I keep circling, avid phantom

R eady for anything, holding on tight, seldom

C learing things by more than a few inches–the trick's not to

L ook down or slow up, keep faking fast, changing

E xpressions to respond to everything even before

I t happens, totally prepared, as if I believed we could all

N ow have something in common & can respond to that feeling,

T elling myself at any moment life is sure to take over, as I'd

H oped it always would, whisk us all away to live in one garden not

E ven a few beats away on angel-wing where

N ot a flower that flares & falters

I s lost when the angel of night appears

G athering hot pearls to hang on her black skin, then

H olding back skirts to reveal a child gripping live coals

T ight, coals under his tongue, staring at you.

A nd you know him, know he can't let go, can't let them drop. So

N ow you take his hand. Together you walk

D own the narrow path where flames lick, and we

A re slowly consumed by fire,

like a tourist

CALENDAR GIRL

The nymph sits in her cave, naked.
The deckchair lusts after the strange trees.
She cups her chin: I love you.
Each evening I return to her though
the divorcee next door who sunbathes on her lawn
has a big chest with a few
black hairs. When I take the nymph to school
& unroll her she says: I love him.
She's keen on sports. Me too. When I get home
I forget I'm tired, but tired I am.
She has that effect. I crawl along my branch
like a chameleon, watching her with my
swivel eyes. My tongue is sticky.
She understands. I watch her try to move.
She twitches. Suddenly she's
outside the window. My fingers open.
Something is undone before it's done.
The divorcee. I stand up so fast I knock
the binoculars off the National Geographics
& onto the floor. Freeze. Turn on the radio.
It shouts something about cold light & old men.
She smelled of skin. I know how to swim.
Voulezvous swimmez avec moi? Ah,
she's left her face in the mirror.
I lick it. She would understand. Now
watch me ride onto your lawns, destroy
your cities, rape your women till they
glint like large diamonds. It starts to rain.
Smell of beans downstairs on the stove.
I look out. She has me
where she wants me.

ARS AMATORIA: CHORUS FOR ST. VALENTINE'S DAY

Strophe

Bird tracks I followed from feeder across snow,
 across snow from feeder bird tracks
that disappeared into chiasmus then reappeared
 from under the book I'd left open as I fell asleep
& hopped into my mind dreaming of time as
 an enormous light inside a bear in his cave
seeming to die, but no, the glamour is still on him,
 while the great sickle rises over him
in a billion billion volts & night wears on
 & great distance & time stops here
where my wife is asleep & naked beside me.

Antistrophe

 In the morning I find myself standing
where the bobcat bit a meadow vole in half,
 her hind legs sticking out of the snow & not a speck
of blood, as if she is coming out of a bloodless dream
 backwards or diving headfirst for figurines
in some wintry wreck. Am I too old for saints?

Strophe

 I am standing again in night up to my waist,
wanting to shout encore to the whole scene
 & mean it, my gray whiskers flaring behind
the woods, silver wire pointing to dwarf stars,
 bloody lips chomping on the white arm beside me,
on the stumps of unreason swollen the way pebbles
 light up underwater to make unthought-of dark flowers.

Antistrophe

The lady lies on clean sheets, eyes scanning the black sea,
 until beside her a seal's face breaks the surface,
opens his mouth, tries to chew sky & spit stars
 like words & music, but what comes out are little birds
making a living, making do, making tracks across the blank page
 of an implausible sky, tracks she follows.

BASSO-RELIEVO

That feeling as a kid—double the limbs,
two of everything, rolled into a ball,
traveling in any direction. That sense
of omnipotence, unblemished by sex
(Aristophanes says people then propagated
like grasshoppers, shed seed in furrows).
Until that sense of omnipotence challenged
the Father, and was cut down to size,
or cut straight down the middle, split
from that primeval state. The surgeon
was that Apollo of reason, moderation,
self-control. Split like a sorb-apple
for pickling. This was the way of humility.
But things did not go well. Loneliness
came into the world, recognition of self
and not-self. And when these halves
found other halves they'd clasp, and not
let go, even though starving, even though
they suffered from self-neglect.
So Zeus moved their sex up front;
some sort of stop-gap, pacifier. That
made things worse. So now we have
knowledge and yearning. And the threat
from on high that if we ever try to
reunite, we will be halved again.
But I am already basso-relievo on
this old tomb. All profile: one leg,
one arm, no back or front, no past or
present, staring ahead in stone.

PAINTING BY ANON

Like stone unconsecrated, I lost
feeling. Clearly, every year
wills us dead. But at the end
of the transept I saw him dancing
as if he didn't have to, and felt
better. Then, like madness,
a coldness interwove again
its sad conjecture until from a
stained-glass tree a body
hung as if it wanted to, fingers
spilling birds and birds, and from
the head fauns and phalloi.
At his feet stiff milkweed sprayed
seeds across the water and behind,
toward the lights, a fish-line snaked out,
and behind that scrolls of nets
from trawlers drifting off.
This is the kind of thing you'd expect
from Etruscan tombs, where death
is life. At Veii, for example, where
I coupled alongside the rock-cut
water courses, the ritual bathing-places
in the woods, beside the tombs,
among the glitterings and purlings,
the jigging scraps of light scattering
like insects, coming back together,
like art contracting and expanding,
pulling together memories of the invented past.

> *"We are occupied by gods. The mistake is to identify with the god occupying you."*
> —Carl Jung

He takes the ivory swan he's been carving
  for weeks and gives it to his daughter. "What's this
for?" she says, laying it aside. Passing through
  a door almost smaller than himself, he walks in dust
where footsteps fade like fishes.
  His wife barely looks over from
flapping laundry held back by wooden pegs.
  A breeze shivers in the bushes. He shivers,
and stops. His bones get up and walk away,
  push on in weather now like a musty attic.
Light shines through him and he cannot stop it.
  He decides to follow to somewhere unpronounceable
where swans can swim back where they came from.

THE ECONOMY OF WINDMILLS

These are just windmills, or images
   of windmills, for now they make nothing,
trading in tourists. We file them away.
   Seen. The sky is blue, the sails blat round
in it, disappearing into themselves.
   There's a power-station down the road
and fields of tulips cavort in a bland mania,
   tulpenwoerde. All's well. It's hard to imagine
Don Quixote tangling with these. At their feet
   a stream makes uncertain progress
over rocks; obstacles fix its pace. I look up:
   turmoil in quiet sky, high in the rack.
 Clavileño couldn't fly there, where the main star
   sails on above the *whump whump whump*,
the whooshing and woolgathering making good time,
   pulling in air, stirring it until dark gets
sucked into the airy trade too, windhandel,
   and is bottomed out, dropping to nothing.
The wind has shared what it could, and,
   has shifted away, speculating in currents
over the North Atlantic, stirring them
   like memories, of desire, or great gain.

AMSTERDAM

In memoriam Leo Lionni

He came at them with his stick,
    fending them off, sending them scurrying
down the long white corridor & out
    onto the green grounds beneath the
Tuscan hills. He had forgotten all
    his stories from all over.
His wife calmed him down, took his cane,
    got him back to bed, still raging,
but quieter. He turned to look for
    the hills, & as he did the mice
he'd whelped & weaned came out
    of their holes bringing him their
little wisdoms in wicker baskets,
    & he tasted each one & spat it out.
Bitter, bitter. The mice scattered.
    He wanted to bite the hills, the
Chianti hills, take chunks out of them,
    leave teethmarks on Porcignano,
its boar-laden woods, the valley
    whose caves hid partisans.
But he lay back. He had heard
    canal water lapping at his feet,
the slap slap slap
    of oars under his window.
He gripped his stick & looked about
    for something to move.

EXIST

As a kid I never thought of "pain" as
    something I felt. What I felt I could not
name or share. Now out the window I watch
    a thin chemical yellow smear being
pushed down by gray rolls of night. Behind me
          the physics of the TV screen

Plays out plots and previews. Outside is shapes
    moving under neon like those who have
already moved on. Lighted windows stick
    in the sky, independent of stone or
brick. I can only exist in writing,
          when for a while I do not know

I "exist." I exist only when I
    don't exist? There I am at the window,
staring back at me, in glass, dependent
    on the dark. In a room beyond this one,
I see myself in replicas that come and
          go with light, most there when most dark.

ESCHATOLOGY

The small body discovers the body dies, but
If it were a blackbird it would come back
Year after year and not stay down.
It is aware the world has seams.

Later yearning in hard dark, she has
The hummingbird fly out of its epidermis
As a lover would to feel the leaving,
And from the peel another bird double back

Into a rainbow. It is lovely, the whole range.
Now it will be alright. The world will race
And glow again like rivers. Imagine: all it takes is,
"What shall I tell myself?" And you have

A photo of a place you've never been
That takes you there, rapt in calm and quiet,
Intense and aureate, part of an evolving
Conversation that includes chasms that close

When you look at them, like in a fairytale,
And open too, done and undone the same,
And what was sitting on your chest
To stop your breath is now a marvel

You can enter as if it were ordinary,
Somewhere in a future that does not punish
But continues in different weather,
Much the same as this.

WHERE THE WOODS BEGIN

In memoriam RGB

My friend is now in dreams,
like the one where I rake a pile of hair
and leave it near the heaped-up grass.
Later, I scare myself so bad, I say:
"I thought the pile of hair a wolf!"
He's there to light it, turn fear
to smoke. And now his ash is planted,
though he wanted to be scattered on the water,
touch everywhere and everyone; those
he dreamed to being, believing the people
could be breathtaking, and Marx right.
His mother would have understood,
she who left her Russian Jewish home
and a husband who beat her when she read;
who joined the Party, washed office floors,
and in her early forties had this son
to a young Catholic priest from Ireland,
whose name she never told. She'd like it
that he lies scrupulously gray,
in an urn wrapped in brown paper,
placed in the last plot left
in the artists' cemetery, in the corner,
where the woods begin.

NERUDA IN PURGATORY

Blue patches of weather; shivered blue stone
  I try to scratch a fire from. A single swallow
balks where red water screeches & an invisible hand
  forces it into progressively narrower spaces.
Somewhere in the search for the useful,
  nuptual matter, there still may be flowers
to pluck from sleepy faces. But not here,
  the proletariat no more than a chronic itch;
not here where a man facing eternal loneliness
  can only shoot out words like pistons,
abandoning gears, staring at the Janus hood-ornament.
  I have been left to starve in a garden,
a jackdaw tacked to the gate, scarf fluttering
  in tacky red clods. I start a fire. Each spark
gropes upward, as if up was the only nourishment.
  They allow me my figurehead in the window
now the world is all shore. A sea-music less
  than half-roar takes up what it can.
I was wrong, I was right. I was left
  here where I devolve into spray, salt, bitter,
unlearned, not yet repentant. No one
  sees the blood in the sand I lay the driftwood over,
and light a match. *Hay tantos muertos....*

from SNOW HOUSE

SNOW HOUSE

ena qanikcaq

*"A Yupik word is not merely a static construct but may approach
a dynamic sentence in microcosm"*
                              – Osahito Miyaoka
"Man is…unshielded"
                              – Martin Heidegger

Sharp edges, rounded off to the
    nearest curve, how many worlds
can you make at random, if
    random is the world seen
in extremis, whole sentences strung
    out, making sense of whatever
each lands on, taking from it,
    giving. Parts of this speech are
everywhere, in flocks and little songs,
    a wild chirping in cochlea and
cloud. And from this houses are made,
    all the same and all different.
Lapidary but loose in syntax it covers
    everything, making itself up as it
goes along, as it falls, loosening
    the land, and tightening it up,
blown this way and that by gust
    and gale, only to pile up and link
with starry burrs on a continent
    of give-back, a whole whirling
world of joists and angles linking
    and renewing, unlike anything and
like everything, more and more itself,
    glass that drops over you
so you shine brighter out.

WITTGENSTEIN'S SCREW

The calendar moves by degrees.
    Someone's finger is pointing at the rain,
at gulls in gray dunes that float up
    into their inverse likeness. There they hover
as torn up clouds over beaches drifting
    with the tide, dancing with it, draping
themselves over so they seem unmoving.
    Then I see a heron by the inlet.
He stands, one thing, unmoved, as if
    cut out from whatever had stood there
before him, exactly filling his space
    so nothing is left over, scissored out
of gray blue sky and cloud, gray blue water
    so the longer you look the more he
disappears until at last what you thought
    some sort of finality, some definitive shape,
is gone, and you look right through to sky
    and water and beyond to gulls marking dunes
like punctuation until they too are released
    into water and cloud, and the ripe rain is turning
and moving straight at you as if it is something,
    and the sky moves on, turning like
Wittgenstein's screw that turns without moving
    any part of the mechanism to which it is attached.

THE SHIELD OF ACHILLES

On it I engrave another scene in which
    I gave them what they wanted, "things
as they are," although it was not mine to give.
    They'd guessed that much, having seen through
my disguise and noticed my limp. They'd take it
    all the same, they said. You never know.
But when they left they didn't—by then I had confessed
    that all I do is forge whatever's needed
with whatever comes to hand, stick things where
    they make or don't make sense, such as here
and now where birds rise over the river's mouth
    then sweep above pines, flexed, looking to be
understood the way the world once was, which
    I still try to do, so that in that seagull's eye
I'd turn vast and burn into things, making something
    that will eventually unmake itself, and so on.
I try a phrase to stamp it into yet another shape
    but something flashes from it like a file of fire ants
and I follow, heading to where more seabirds have returned
    to sit on an old wreck, staring at the sky as if
it was something on its own, not theirs. Then
    something spooks them and they take off into the curve
of the horizon I blow on until a flame erupts that,
    passing, leaves black streaks on clouds and along
the sides of this house like the ocean's mark when it
    withdraws to flow around the edge of the shield which is
the world which could be you but isn't, ever, quite.

BIRDS IN THE WOODS

Silence is involved in itself as
    loads of light float down white
as the flames that lighted on
    the disciples with the gift
of tongues. Just after dawn,
    I'm waiting for sleep to unravel
just enough so I can speak
    in a voice still not mine, one
perhaps like the carpenter's
    down the road who makes
models that may not look
    like much you recognize,
but work. What does it take
    to scrap the patterns and
start again? There are things
    I know but have never seen
or heard, syllables self-effacing,
    interlocking but not quite
consistent, solid, but not quite
    there. I like it when culverts
trail after the streams they're
    built to contain; when after
storms great cords of water
    interweave, or get torn apart
again but you wouldn't know it.
    It could be the same thing,
forces forming and reforming.
    When the time comes I'd
like to be something like that.
    Things will continue to wear
themselves out, but still
    be standing. Birds will sing
in the woods but the woods
    will be gone.

COYOTE

neat in brown & gray, boater at an angle
    on his head, airing his quiff, coming to consume
my deckchairs & gardening equipment, pick my moonflowers
    & my wife, rolling down my path like water
until, seeing me, the turn & conflagration of his tail
    dries him up at once. That spring, I'd found traces
of transcendence along that path, poked it with a stick
    to see what went into it. But now—the Ding an sich!
Or was it? Like Red Riding Hood with my blueberry basket
    on my arm, I continued on my way, unsure of what
I'd seen. Perhaps I'd read too much. I moved
    cautiously out into my field that was now mine
no more, flowing down south-east like the alluvial silt
    it once was, until a quick stir in the grass almost
made me jump into my basket, go with the flow.
    I closed my eyes. When I opened them—nothing. Just
wooded mountains, empty path, blueberries like little bells
    ringing right & left, pines counting the days &
whispering, & over all wind sounding the All Clear,
    just like when I was a kid & the sirens signalled the
temporary end to doodlebug & shrapnel. So, all clear
    on a dog-day afternoon, keys falling back to minor,
I settled down to a domestic picking. But as I moved
    from patch to patch I felt little flames flicker &
a smell like glass flowed in from clumps of willowherb
    & hardhack. I stood, waiting to hear, perhaps,
a yodel from the other side of the wall &
    scatter the cows, set off the dogs, make the farmer
look up in my direction & go get his shotgun. But
    nothing. So I climbed the wall. Was I the only one
could smell the smoke, feel the rush of wind, see
    a shadow like a gunshot? And then I heard
a deeper breath. Was that me breathing, an air so cool
    & local I wouldn't need to speak for some time?
A tree flared, & the blue sky showed a white half-moon
    with half a crazy gray face in it as if the rest

of the body was too light to stay. Then, way off in a
   dark stand of spruce & hemlock a yelp, a clatter,
a hawk, a gargle. Suddenly, a whole band was up there,
   tuning up, then slowly sliding into a kind of
celestial circular breathing, all held together by
   a swooping tenor sax. They ran through a few numbers,
stumbled, struggled, collapsed, ending in a silence
   like the sound after the toilet has finished flushing,
the tank full, fresh water settled. And all the birds
   started up again like I'd never heard before.

TAMIAS STRIATUS POETICS

"The poem is a sort of animal"
— Ted Hughes

I give him words to tell me who he is.
   He gives them back, begins a visual discourse
on invisibility, gunning by me a film in snippets &

   jump-cuts, starring him. Light flashes everywhere.
But you can still make out frames that form a sequence,
   though there are deep lacunae only he can leap

as a kind of semiotic stuntman–I guess it's him, though
   it could be a series of doubles (impossible to know).
There–in that shot he's signifying a signified, so

   in what follows he's multiple as the seeds he collects
like mnemonics. There, off he goes again, but now in a
   series of silent sequences subtitled: "The Vital Nothing,"

"The Plump Filling," "The Cake of Soap," "The Full Stop,"
   &, dramatically, "Tamias Striatus Meets Pale Ramon."
He's starting to blur like a piece of stained air, or

   something identical. But to what? Himself? He cuts a
dashing solipsism, so comparisons are useless. Now he's
   riding a fast vehicle. He is a vehicle. But of what?

Himself? Here we go again... I'm about to call him accident
   & let it go at that, but suddenly a small yet purposeful charge
goes off & something claps shut after itself, closing me out.

   All I can hear is a series of fingersnaps, fragments of old songs,
theatrical effects that burrow into worlds & then pop up again,
   now here, now there, more believable the more you believe.

Clearly, he's an idea whose time has come & gone almost
   in the same instant, an ironic reading that can't quite
cancel itself out. So this reader's response is to have him stay

as he is, whatever that is, in that moment when I can say
he's there, because as soon as I say he isn't he jumps out
   of my head, skitters off fingertips, skirrs just behind my heels,

& off we go again. He's turning me inside out, in circles, stripping
   my defences. He's–wait! There he is! He's there! What you see is
what you get. But what have I seen? Sometimes you can think

   too much. I give in. He knocks me out.

CHIPMUNK

If, as Kit Smart said, toads have compensation
    for being toads, "since there are stones whose
constituent particles are toads," this particular
    Algonquian helps constitute a granite range
whose high inflections interweave. He flows
    between subject and object, neither and both.
He is, as the linguists say, non-configurational,
    and like the wind up there no one can tell
whence he came or where he goes. He's all
    action, all tiny jerks whose frames overlap
so quick they almost look seamless, impulses
    received and renewed just about at the
same time and at the same fast speed but
    as if that is too slow and he could go faster
if he really tried. Impulse and impulse,
    each thought an impulse tried successfully
many times over. Try saying him.
    Try thinking him with no words.

LIGHTNING-FLASH-BEING

Hunched over controls, engine like fingers
running through a comb, a bolt of Blakean delight
aiming straight at Urizen, voice the lightning's voice, electric,
sun emblazoned on each wing, tail fins forked like antennas
to catch and amplify the cosmos, multi-colored prayer-sticks
stuck in his hair.... He balks, almost out. Fuels up again
to take it out on air, chocks away, a backflip à la Olga Korbut—
he drives as if driven by some deep-seated slight, real or imagined,
dropping color like foil to elude eyes, shooting off, buzzing
himself in glass, chasing himself away, poking his nose
into any business, even mine, on the porch before seven,
a smear of sun on my head that's some sweet thought
weaiting for inspection and probe from this extraterrestrial
who's just crossed the solar system & is now climbing vertically,
dropping at breakneck speed, then shooting off
at ninety degrees since g-forces don't apply
in this deep New Mexico sky as hospitable to
flying saucers as hummingbirds—though the former
have crashed here and their baby-faced dead
carted off for inspection, these guys never crash,
their technology more advanced, making every color
count, created out of blank by minds that split
the time/space continuum. However, if one ever does
come down, and if someone does step out alive,
you can bet he won't have goggle-eyes and skin like wax. No—
nose long as a flute, pack on his back full of who knows
what wonders; clad not in dull aluminum but a sun-suit
dazzling to the eye, with something to say that will
amaze us, not just for what he has to tell,
but the way in which he tells it.

EGG

"We are in the position of defining myth by the shape of its absence."
– Sean Kane, *Wisdom of the Mythtellers*

The bluebird's cold mistimed egg
fetched up from the one-legged
   box after the pair had left for
points south & unknown (never,
   as it turned out, to return)
I renested in the half-geode by
   the windowsill where it gleamed
&, months becoming years, seemed
   about to last forever, holding its pure
blue firmament up over what by now
   was nothing, till one January day, snow
melting to a fast flood,
   I blew it softly onto my palm so I could
hold its cerulean up against new sky,
   home against home, where it lay
weightless & delicate as the Xmas ornament
   we'd just put away, but when I went
to roll it gently back onto its bed,
   & leave it there, I saw a thread,
a crack, another, watched it sink in
   slowly on itself, shard on shard collapsing
from my touch & breath, relaxing
   into the shape of its absence.

THE COW AND THE WALL

Up on former pastures cows once climbed & snorted
at something poking out at them, large trees now fly till they
run out of air, & the mountain itself tugs
out its roots, shedding bits of itself like bark
or hair caught on snags of a rough June sky.
But on the lower slopes cows still clamber about in fields
they keep clear with deer who lead them astray into corn-patches,
or, like the Holstein heifer Bailey, leap
over walls to get at fallen apples on my land,
where I watch her snip and slurp till they go off
in her four stomachs like time-bombs quenched by pails
of gasoline so she takes off after herself
where she had last seen herself, trying to jump
back over the walls backwards & logical, again & again,
bellowing for me to put things back the way they were
when everything worked, turn things around
so she'll know what was where by what had been there.
Soon she's jumping backwards, expecting to go forward,
her rubber shoes hitting the flat stone keys,
accompanying herself in a low moan till the northern lights
go off in her eyes & the stones all round begin to
call out from their ancient depths, an echo to her grand
confusion of mind, as if together they can solve
how place can stay the same yet reach
different conclusions until after a while it seems
as if the wall is wailing & the cow
jumping in place like a wall trying to clear itself,
growing less convinced it is making progress, going
from a place it no longer wants to a place
it can no longer reach & loving the world.

THE PRINT

Sometimes I'm someone else, like–berserk.
I've been kicked off busses, bounced
from places I wouldn't be seen dead in,
and once left for dead in a Wal*Mart
parking lot. Tonight the house I'm paying off
is his, the air prickly & thunder still
on the prowl so my flesh crawls.
Sky's so close I could hook it &
drag it down to see what's there,
just like the bear last night who came
out of nowhere & pulled over the stump
hauled from the woods last spring
to paint "Arthur and Ursula" on,
except now there's no Ursula.
Morning showed the rotted stump in shreds,
ants milling about in shock, their world
gone, some legless, some clamped
onto corpses, no idea which end was up,
nowhere home any more. Nothing else
was touched, not a leaf out of place,
as if to make a point, the only other sign
one flat footprint left carefully in the middle
of an old anthill at the side of the driveway
leading down and out but which
on closer inspection turned out to be my own.

A DREAM OF THE PREHISTORIC

They come out dry, stretch & sing,
Let's see, chestnuts, yours and mine,
then divide & share them like crowns.
God knows they know gods. Scents
are a shade they sit under, while
a wolf gets used to their whistling.
In the hut made of, what, mastodon
tusks, reindeer antlers, branches & trunks?
they keep getting bigger. The baby
wrapped in skins & poppies is stretched
on a slate, while his older brother is
already turning to bearded pony, wisent,
bird on a stick, salmon swimming upstream
criss-crossed with moon marks.
Everyone dreams, & the threads are used
for everything they wear, or, decomposed,
the physical moment itself. A loud noise
could be thunder, or the sound that
turns them inside-out as they live
at the heart of echoes, everything touching,
and *see* means *understand*, and
understand means what it says.
But it's not so much the dream
they turn to or into; rather it's
the somewhere else that goes with them,
breaking open fire so it sticks
to the walls of caves as ochre hands
blown wide, & leading deeper from
space to space turning everything
into the lamp of a reason that's
dangerous as the tusk in the spine
or a landslide. Meanwhile, the bird-
headed man is numberless & disappears
in front of eyes that see him climb
like a lark up the tree whose rungs ring,
& see him return again & stay on the

flickering walls. He is the one who
wakens them into another dream where,
dazed by the everyday, everyone could
be everything & everything come down
out of the rock, out of the rock's
brown nipples, everything slippery to
the touch, & disembodied hands
grasp beginning & end at once, swimming
over each other. But then,
one day the bell rang, sun blared,
& survivors huddled together to tell
their stories & sing their songs in fits
& fragments. When I got there,
I just had time to find a few hand-puppets
& ivory carvings, figurines in coal,
before the authorities impounded my plane
& locked me up.

CARMEN MIRANDA'S HAT

He peers out, parting the ferns. He is ready again
to love someone, perhaps construction workers,
perhaps ashcans and pigeoncoops on tar beaches,
if he can find them. He walks through shale & granite,
between, on one side, a swamp with big things in it,
& on the other a sandbank along which treads a silky path
leading to a few rows of corn & ginko trees with fruit
that sits on the ground like vomit & a mushy spring
feeding a stream with trout quick as laughter &
a coke bottle tinkering with the sun so he
has to put his hand across his striped face to shade
his painted eyes to see whatever might come through
the sandhills that squeeze the wind so it starts at him
like a flint-head. Now he knows who has passed that way,
urinating in the stream, scratching names on trees,
& who might well again in the foulness of time,
splashing ashore like lost seals, waving cloth & iron pots.
Give me your skins. He moves forward slowly
on what could have been feet, breathes hard, redoubles
his efforts, pushes through scrubby sumac, stubbing his toes
on dumb turtles, the smell of clean sand still in his nostrils.
He wants to tell them Good News, say You are welcome, welcome,
& share again the bounty on Carmen Miranda's hat, pass it around,
tropical, exotic. Here, eat my hat, eat my clothes,
sure, eat my skin, eat me. But they are not there,
maybe never were, unless, he thinks, they are lost somewhere
wandering about like marshgas, disappearing like bullfrogs
into their own harsh voices that never could sing &
their eyes may still be out there, though they cannot see me,
wanting me to find them, afraid as they wonder
how anything can be so still & empty, so quiet,
not even the tremor on a twig, as they race through space,
hair slicked back, white-knuckled, hanging on, not knowing
where they're headed. He pities them, but now he's alone
feels again the dew-claw beginning to push through his skin,
hears the whine and whisper of stars sleeping like bears,

gets scents from folds in the wind, time rotting in the breeze
coming from the great river's front door. This was
the world they'd wanted; they'd also wanted its opposite.
What they took crumbled. Now he sits on what remains
of a rock they made in a place they'd created to look
as natural as possible, even burying in the process
one of their own villages to make a great meadow,
& he watches the huge screen, his eyes projecting all
they can imagine & all they know, & then some, for where
they were concerned there was always the improbable
if not the impossible & he has to leave room for that
& the unimaginable for they were big on the unimaginable,
& as he watches he goes around tasting flowers again,
native & foreign-born the same to the tongue that had tasted
macaw & elephant, camel & tiger, giant sloth & mastodon, and,
in truth, had tasted a few of them from time to time–bitter, bitter.
He practises the few words they taught him & he remembers
because you never know. Yes, he says, you are welcome to my hat.
It is a nice hat, always in season & it will feed you for ever
if you sing & wear it properly. For it is the goddess
Carmen Miranda's hat, on loan. She's going to want it back.

THE MIRRORING

They put up steel. Take
it down. Glass, one minute up,
the next in pieces.
On a dark blue day with
the content of the sea sweeping
through, crying, one minute
it's there, the next not.
Sky's a blank to torture &
drop. When I was young
it seemed answerable. Now
it's level when you look at it
but when you look away it's
folds & pleats you can get
lost in, & if you crawl inside
it has all the appeal of a root-
cellar. But where are the roots?

I stand in the light of our high
back field among wild thyme whose
purple scent knocks you off your feet,
heat rising from rocks no one could move
into walls, & I'm all cracked up, looking
off rocks into blue up down around,
at my feet, far as the eye can see,
& I make a cloud St. Theresa in
ecstasy, the mind turning in on
itself, which is to say out, going
out, breaking up & in each part
& in the breaking a new up
& down, in & out, far & near all
strung together & along by something
like birdsong, something like wind
inside that song that bends notes
like light for as much as it can take
& then mirrors itself with you in the middle
doing much of the mirroring.

CANON 501

The song was moist, filing away,
    drifting while we drifted, something
in blackface, Al Jolson of birdland,
    not quite right, prophesizing until hoarse
who knows what. The locals say he
    draws poison from you, *angatkuk*,
shaman, though they don't believe it.
    Then the incongruous smell of
chrysanthemum crossed us up and
    we remembered the service-station
with someone in handcuffs. Probably
    a mistake, said the attendant, though
they do get violent. The prisoner yawned.
    Our map lumbered from point to point
as if trying to remember something itself,
    anything. We tossed it and got out.
On the long walk back the tundra looked cosier
    by moonlight, everywhere the same,
white as bleached whalebone. But
    things had not been right all day.
In the damp heat everything was wobbly,
    even the bride at the old mission who
seemed to grow clouds like companions,
    drawing them after. I glimpsed a ring
of seal-fur flash on her wrist. *Mm-hmm,*
    unh-hunh they went. The honeymoon
was spent beyond the rigs. It was enough
    for them it didn't rain or snow though
the driftwood fire they made beside the boats
    was all smoke. The sea sounded obscure
as if it had no shape and was empty.
    We tried to capture it on Canon 501
and sent it south, but even that seemed staged.

ALEUT REVERIE

Beyond the other lights, a stumbling
   bodiless light, and then from white water
whiter water, and a brighter light.
   There isn't much to tell me what it is
from these high cliffs where from time
   to time I've stumbled over old green
skulls or weathered bones. The spray
   flies up and I duck, as I used to under
the camera's black cloth to see the land
   and ocean tossing in the sleep of
the Moon's sister as she looked down
   on young men in kayaks, wood visors
prickly with sea-lion whiskers blowing out
   like wisps of smoke as they paddled past
the Evening Star, past Bundles-of-Codfish
   and the Caribou, heading away, away....
And I head back, turning away from the
   light on the sea that's now flickered
out, back toward the sound of one
   hesitatant drum almost drowned
in a radio's slow drone.

POST-INDUSTRIAL

The old slopes flap like muslin.
    Snow gleams as if angels were
reinventing themselves as snow.
    These mountains point to themselves
as if they were photos so you'll know
    they're really there. At their foot,
flashes like a fire going out above
    the railway bridge that hasn't
seen a train in decades. The bent rails
    are their own cargo they carry
from nowhere to nowhere else.
    Yet even from here you can hear
the wind strumming rusted struts.
    In days' deep grain sounds scrape by,
steel-ribbed, all spirit. The bridge is
    now a model of itself moving on staves
to the steady beat of invisible valves,
    driving into the horizon and down
the other side where there are no
    narrow ways, just damp grass and
a sky that smells of pitch, going all ways
    at once without the burden of direction.

PEDAGOGICAL

It rained all week, but the ground's dry.
   I wake and dress. On the far side of the house
a backhoe coughs into life. Summer's short here.
   One sweep of the ax and it's gone, back into stars
that clip these hills with cold edges. These first fall nights
   something is pushing over stones big as tables,
tossing them about, turning walls and paths primeval.
   When asked, I am full of theories, this and that,
probably that. And let it go. This morning, crossing
   the street, our one street, run-down Victoria houses
with porches fuller than the rooms, I make out
   a blue haze brimming from the graveyard.
But after grabbing a bite at Boomagoo's Eatery
   I'm ready for anything. When I enter the classroom,
for once my students seem ready, or at least they're quiet.
   So I take a risk, and talk about poetry. I get
carried away, telling them how a poem floats,
   and opens its mouth, how poetry is an animal
and turns everything animal, gives everything breath,
   and fills it with rhythms like our own. I write one
on the board and tell them it's about a place like this
   by someone who lives in a place very much like this.
I read it out, twice, then, turning back to them,
   repeat it by heart. For once, they are listening.
And watch as I take the poem down, lay it on the stream
   now in full spate at the foot of the desk, float it
off like a leaf or curled bark, and we all see it flash and
   turn and dive in bright water stained with run-off
from the parking lot and the last dairy-farm left,
   heading for the river, which we can now hear
as if for the very first time.

ST. THERESA SAYS

I am fire & plucked chicken, both.
Footprints on a dry riverbed, shadows on the bank.
I am brown hands flapping in a monsoon, shipwrecked near
Dido's palace & a Coca Cola stand. In my pocket is a poem
by Pierre Reverdy I was learning by heart until
the director said *cut*. I am Tollund man who died
in joy, strangled, his mind a kind of honey,
his stomach sprouting grains. I am a young girl's
scented letter to the world. I am that girl's legs
jiggling under her desk, her pen describing what
she has not yet known, while in the distance
presents are being unwrapped & flowers sparkle like eels
in shallows. I am that distance blown up to show
lemon trees filtering something from the air &
returning it to darkness like a gift. I am proud as charity;
dreaming of a love taking hold like a sailor's song.
But flesh is a shade I only sit in, naked, by a low fire,
while a consoling star traces a blue mark down
my chest, & onto my thigh, a shadow like a reed.
One wavering line circles my breasts, & falls
down my back like water. There's a bite mark
on my lip, & another on my hand. God alone suffices.

BARN BURNING

Like a red cypress towering over the gables, sparks fast stars,
   and the flames blowing upward, a madness, the insistent madness
that goes away briefly, dies down, drops down the far side,
   then comes back up refreshed to push out like a light into
the darkness and gives darkness a false depth, as if,
   if you ever went far enough it would turn into something else
too bright to look at, something that shows you yourself
   as you really are, the other side of the way decades have
shaped up and shaped you, not the way you really are,
   not the way you are now, as if you could pull on a new skin,
jubilant and sweet-smelling. Pines sway in the gusts the flames make,
   not the wind. The barn roof's intwisted, caught up,
and little white flames run up and down the long spine
   like flashing water too cool to do any damage. An old barn,
newly gutted and rebuilt, almost done, almost a new thing,
   if that's possible, or the filled-in frame of a desire starting
from the roof, then the sides. Now the tiles are falling down
   the flanks and the flanks collapsing ribs into insides you can
only guess at, what was meant for what, what did what,
   how it worked. But there's a logic here, a shape of destruction
you could figure out, given the context, and though the dry grass
   all round is catching and going off in all sorts of directions
so the mind cannot take it all in, even against the breeze
   fed by the fire, going to where it wants, without forethought,
spitting great gobs with the gusts fire itself is creating,
   and now it is all involved, and no one coming to put it out
this far in, miles from anywhere, and I am the only watcher.
   I watch. I could use the phone but it's down. So
I watch and wait to see what will happen I couldn't predict,
   see if when it all collapses there is relief in the air, if things
go on as before, if anyone notices, if there is anything left
   to relate to, anything that survived to be built on from the
ground up, or if it is too late and what I'd watched was all
   there was, just a burning down, or if what was there is still there,
a shape etched into night, a spectral afterimage, its contour
   clear as it had been before, so you can close one eye and trace it

with a finger, blurring the sharp edges, pitch of roof, where the wall
    turns and points to the well-house and the rows of cypresses
once lining the driveway, and it will follow your finger, trailing
    off it, moving where it moves, stopping when it stops until
you point and shake it off, still living, or drag its brilliant line
    only you can draw over fields and sky, the line only you
can read, taking it all again to what it was but not where,
    or there and somewhere else, when all I really wanted was
to have it nowhere, but nowhere's always somewhere and this thing
    seems sworn to keep me, burning my outline around me,
consuming me, burning me up to go out in a plume of glory,
    taken off somewhere, dispersed in a different form, broken down
into particles that scatter like bright seeds, like thoughts, fire
    a knife replacing every part and organ with something shining,
not here but everywhere, going in at my eyeballs and ears,
    deep into lungs that had dried to the skeleton of a leaf,
moving around inside until the features stand out against
    the night sky like a jubilee, the flare of a single match.

WALKING ACROSS THE ROOM

Our bodies are cast to think themselves everywhere,
  relentless as air, sternward, to stars, bellying

in the dark, sumptious even on stone where they're
  just shadow, each moment a short scene, a shawl

of white water drifting in low through things
  while the soul, incandescent, but as here as bread,

is a kind of billowing breaking up in flashes.
  This way hearts break the better to support themselves.

In its shade we hear the murmur of shade, like birds rising
  in fountains. The body is now complete. Naked,

I am introduced to myself, walk across the room
  my steps lamps as, like a hawk, the dark

turns and swoops, making it hard still to breathe
  on my own, but I breathe.

from IN LATE LIGHT

WORLDS

Air is empty. It's empty.
We fill it with absence. The piano plays
a few bars, then goes quiet. The sun pounds on
the sea and windows stretch
to breaking point when they will let in
a madman who will tell us what we've all
agreed does not exist.
He walks into a patch of brightness
and fractures into blossom which is how
he'll be remembered. He will return
years later for the fragments he left
under our skin. With these he'll make more worlds
closer than skin where
the sun gathers itself into raindrops
at the end of pine-needles, hanging there, heavy,
turning to branches in
night sky so we can touch the moon
and collect the stars and say: "How many
worlds we have!"

There is a clearing by a certain stone
where images flow and are worth stopping for.
   I have stayed there almost all day in silence
until night remembered what belonged to it
   and its shadows started to take back its own.
I've found it hard to walk away as starlight
   infused daisies and the stone itself began
to feel like a star so, although what I have done
   with my life isn't much, for a while
it seemed to be in line.

ROCKS

In late light leaves
flick & fish

stare up before
drifting away. I am

not thinking. I'm
watching these

rocks burn at
a thousand points

so you could believe
they have nerves, skin

you can see through,
their freight anguish,

their rhythm patience,
as their shadows fall

& soon they fall
into their shadows

with the sound, if
they could make

a sound, of waves
falling down over

themselves forever

TRANSUBSTANTIATION

If we only knew how fireflies are
    long-tailed or short-tailed stars
or even not stars at all but
    lemons dying of thirst, pleading
like sucklings, or soldiers at a
    water-hole smelling of cumin,
feverish on the black wet stones
    so no wonder they look confused
through the flowers and wire
    as little lights go off in their heads
and on their tongues when they
    dive at lightning on the water or
leap up at wandering celestial wheels
    that cast no shadow so they can't
be lost, always where they are going
    in a wide wake, always on the
other side of things, or how they're
    gold of the conquistadores melting
in gouts drifting away, then we might
    know the true substance is not ash
or accident but what's left is still
    the real thing so, though we may not
know what that is, there's no point
    in trying not to catch it.

THIS PLACE

There is a proper season for stars, and enough
    time for the abyss. On this granite floor,
however, nothing is certain, not even the
    little song I thought I heard, disembodied,
almost anonymous. It could have been
    a poppy head in the display case. Or maybe
a cuckoo. I counted the notes as if counting
    was a virtue, and even sang a few notes
in a register useful for grasshoppers,
    but it was lost on them. Today, everything
is lost, probably due to the posture gods
    used to warm their thighs which tended
to the crushing of mortals, So now, gigantic
    on the wall, their shapes are flickers or fever.
Somewhere may be another world, but I have
    chosen this place for the echoes. I stand
behind the lemons on the table as if summoned,
    thinking of fishes tossed into a boat. I have
set aside their shiny shadows and will wait to see
    how to use them. Whatever they are like
I'll call mine. I have gathered other things
    too, indifferent to quality, setting necessity
next to impoverishment. And even if all this
    never existed it will appear as something
by which I'll make my way. If when I wake
    nothing's there I'll want that too.

TEMENOS

Some forty years ago when I was young
    everything seemed quid pro quo and
feasible even if it wasn't. You could
    grow wise on compulsions or
convert on a whiff. Things aren't
    that way now—at least that's what
I was thinking as I opened the gate
    to a patch of sunlight and stepped into
the shade, of which there was too much,
    but this was the only possible place
for a garden in the woods. I'd dug it out
    from red hard-pan and rock around
the house I never thought I'd own,
    filled it in with whatever seemed right,
wood-duff, leaves, potash, kitchen scraps
    and scavenged worms, buckets of manure
hauled from the farmer's field at night,
    whatever came to hand. I never went
to garden school. And now life is heaping
    underground, thrusting up at me, leaping
and heading out like fire, which it is,
    a slow fire, pushing past me out the gate
and fence designed to keep it in,
    caught up in its own possibilities,
even the possibilities of collapse, fruiting
    into capitals and cornices, volutes
and friezes and irregular dancing meters,
    singing a wide-awake sleep of many colors
that envelope and embody you so even
    when you close the gate it's never closed

AS IF

"The days of our years are threescore years and ten…"

Psalms 90:10

"Seventy years I regard as the limit of the life of man…"

Herodotus, *Histories*, I

At my age I should be dead, I think as I walk
among heirlooms under a moon that rocks
and wallows, a ship on the rocks, caught in a swell
that drives her further on, scattering bullion

and moidores. At my age I stay in one place,
and here I am with tomatoes that seem to eat the dark.
I move among them like, I say, mountain water.
They are listening. I am listening. We could be

turning to mountain music as leaves stir, we could
be waiting for the stones to reverberate, stars
start to whistle as they climb over themselves, swinging
about like the seas, and I say, Now you can let me in,

as the fruit moves to its own rhythm, spreading
over the ground, escaping wires and stakes,
mimicking the orange moon, taking it in so
their seeds stir, unbounded as night. They could

be remembering resurrections, being brought back,
while I remember the rockpools of my childhood coast
teeming with fish I reached in for, the threnody
of ocean waters like cornets or conch-shells for the

coronation of cardinal or Aztec emperor, *tlatoani*,
or the Buddhas I now walk among, plump, fulfilled,
self-lit incumbents of sun and moon. In their perfume
I move as if forever, as if there were no "as if."

CLICK SONG

For the last few days I've thought I was going mad or about to die, something
going off in my head, my chest, everything caught in the glare of an intense sun,
after my wife of thirty years was told she had cancer, so I've listened to
every word she's said, recording syllable by syllable, in slow motion, when even
to pass her empty book-basket at the bottom of the stairs is a sign as sharp
as that shotgun's blast, those over-ripe tomatoes left on the vines, the bloated squash
and the broccoli gone to flower, even the chipmunk's call from the bluestone slab
we brought from our dead friend Ray's place and laid on top of the wall as if it grew there,
her call that rebounds from everywhere so if you couldn't see her you wouldn't know
where she was though sometimes I almost think she's my wife, as when
they stretch out on the deck, one on her back listening to her iPod, the other
on her front listening to the wind, and I tell the chipmunk but not my wife
that I think I'm about to die or going mad as she sits by her burrow dug into
the side of the house and looks at me and I look back, talk to her as if that
can prevent anything bad from happening and as I walk round the garden
I talk to myself to keep calm, and talk to her again whether she's there or not
or to anything within earshot who will listen because today I feel I might die
and I should leave this record in case nobody remembers me except this chipmunk
who really seems to know my voice and value it and who it seems always appears
when I think of her and often when I don't, who is always in good health
and knows where she's going, who flows down the steps like water, who looks
at me with black pupil-less eyes, singing her healing click-song from the bluestone slab,
her whole body shaking, putting everything into it, and I try to believe her.

FOR AN ANONYMOUS THRUSH

"For he can tread to all the measures upon the music"
      – Christopher Smart, *"Jubilate Agno"*

For I will consider nobody's bird, this song-thrush
Who is nobody's servant but serves all,
Who for years I have thanked each spring and summer day
Often as I lay on my bed looking out at the trees,
Thinking this and that, and year after year hearing his song,
Immortal bird, as one brief thing, or a few notes, however lovely,
On a string, and then, just a few days ago for the first time
Paying close attention, discovering each phrase to be
Its own bubble and variation, theme of variations,
Quick bell-notes with frays and furbelows, like something
The wind might make if the wind had mind.
For just as recently after, as I say, taking him for granted,
I have watched him closely as he hopped in the small ditch
I dug along my garden to carry off the storm-water,
Of which there is a lot, and where he sometimes takes
An earthworm or maybe two for his pains though
It's taken me for ever to persuade them to see my plot
For what it is, organic, and make it home, and I'd prefer
He ate the plain brown ones, not those with blue stripes.
For I will consider this bird that flew across my garden
This morning just as the rain began to darken the windows
So they became a mirror, or invisible to him, just a
Quicker way across to the other side. For that was when
I heard the bang and saw small feathers floating
Down silently to where he lay on his right side,
One small black iris-less eye staring up at me
Blinkless, and I thinking, Oh, he's dead. But then,
He'll come around. They often do. They have
Miraculous powers to heal themselves. And so
I waited. But he still lay, and the cold rain
Soaked his feathers. And therefore I will consider
This wood-thrush who was a good wood-thrush,
Doing what wood-thrushes do, nothing spectacular
Apart from his singing, but spectacular nevertheless,
With strong wings and a breast covered with dots like ermine,

A singer of songs and eater of flies that bite the flesh
And caterpillars that eat cabbages, and all manner
Of other noxious insects, finding them tasty,
As well as a fat worm or two which I don't begrudge,
Who bothered nobody for when he didn't sing he was silent
As he went about his days and endured his nights
Without complaint, who blended in, within his heart
Just the wish to be a thrush and make more thrushes
just like him by singing well.
For he took great joy in his singing, harmonizing
With himself, from the first glance of the glory in the east
Or when dark and cloudy with the threat of rain.
For he kept things straight by keeping on.
For he needed no instruction since he listened carefully.
For he preened his wings as if conferring a blessing.
For he counteracted the Devil, who is Death,
By brisking about his life, though the Devil has
The last word.
For he was an instrument for children to learn music upon,
Though now the house is incomplete and woods barren.
For now the song has broken, gone back to earth.
For this is not good to think on.
For I had said his powers failed.
For the fact that this is not so.
For his powers which earlier I had said failed
Have not. For I checked and checked again until
Two hours and then gave up. And then I checked some more,
The last time rolling back with my hand the tall grass
Where he had fallen. He was not there. The space was empty
And he had gone.
And in the rain a new song like those I'd heard before
But louder, at the same time further off while
Close at hand.
And for I do not have to lie again to my wife and child
When they ask if the bird really did what I said, and did
It all turn out right.
For it did.

HATHOR

Life was ordinary then, and I was
ordinary too, a kid. And the cows
were ordinary though each was
a totally different breed, unique,
or no breed at all, picked up
here and there, a mish-mash.
But each had her name, and I
had one too though sometimes
I took theirs, Liz or Vi, Cushie,
Hackie, I had many to choose from,
and sometimes I ate what they ate,
sweet grass stems, or cubed cow-cake,
rich and oily, delicious, and
sometimes I drove them from
byre to burn, walking behind
their hammock-hips, their
easy functions, when summer
nights still depended on stars
which gave us our first gods,
cows and bulls, and which
I could still make out in their
blue-black pastures and watch
until the bombers came for
the mines and shipyards.
After that, milk tasted of fish
and I spat it out for the cows
were now cooped up and fed
fish heads. But they still weren't
safe and I would seldom again
see wide-horned Hathor without
seeing her fields torn apart
and stars shunted aside by
searchlights or blotted by barrage
balloons in nights of sirens and
flames, pummeled by shrapnel.

PEEL

I read that in this famous person's poems "she searches
for signs of what lies beneath and beyond the self."
Which seems to me pointless, as if you wouldn't know

whether to paint with egg tempera or eat it. At eighteen
I came across Tolstoy's "What Is Art?" where he said
an artist is different from other people because instead

of eating an apple he paints it. Even then I thought why
can't he paint it and then eat it, the way at eight, the war
just over, I stood shoeless in line in the snowy playground

where one of the kids was handing out something that turned out
to be small pieces of orange peel, something exotic we'd never
seen before, which I smelled, nibbled, and finally ate for this poem.

LILY

Heading out down our dusty road
I thought: who wears cameos today,
or nylons with seams, or powders
her face with a pink puff kept
in a silver case, or wears a veil,
or elbow-length gloves, and who
gathers blackberries and filberts
from the side of the road or bothers
with apples from trees gone wild?
Heading back up our dusty road,
past another abandoned farm,
wondering if the scabby apples
in my pockets were once
Swaar or Sweeting, Niack Pippin
or just plain Pippin, I'm wakened
by gold flecks lifting ahead and
snagging on the telephone thin
as the chain with its namesake
enamel lily my mother always
gave me to wear under my shirt
every time I had to do something
frightening or dangerous. I watch
the finches clog the line that
brings her words over thousands
of miles, frightened, old, sick,
alone, "What is to become of me?"
and think because of this
what will become of me?

MANGOES

To even touch the tongue to them's to
                              taste something like
              the eternal, or what could pass
for it, certainly the unique, the not-to-be-
              forgotten, but a few too many bites
                              cloy which it's
              doing now, dripping on this
page that's trying to understand a thing or two
              including death, the comedy of death,
                              which ticks even closer
              today, my birthday, August 13,
Venus' Day in the old Roman calendar, so what,
              and a few days after my mother died, her last
                              gargled words over
              the water, after "Why don't you come
to see me?," *I love you,* as the seconds and minutes
              ticked by, as the clock ticks and chafes now so
                              I am thinking of converting
              to a tree, that white pine
outside my study window, for instance, that was
              a stick when I bought this house and now over-tips
                              the roof, blocking my view
              of mountains so I may have to top it
but know I won't since March's ice storm did some
              of that for me, and I feel pity, pity
                              for the tree, so why not
              for my mother who brought me into
this world, though if consulted it might have been against
              my wishes, but now I'm at the other end
                              I may reverse positions
              though it is not up to me,
as it isn't for the pine that's still pushing upward
              with the ambition, maybe, even wounded, of
                              being a mainmast in
              His Majesty's Navy, although there isn't
a navy any more that needs such masts, and to which

we can say "God save," as to my mother sailing
                    now somewhere out
            of light if not of mind or hailing
distance, beyond the transatlantic cable, beyond "I'm sorry"
          though I'm not sure what for, and hope she can
                        forgive me for whatever
              I need forgiveness for, as I
forgive her for not being able to be other than she was,
            and for saying "I love you" and for me saying
                        the same when I didn't know
              why or what good it did since
words mean something different each time they're said, or
          something different to each side, which
                        is what words were made for,
            to be able to say one thing and mean
another, or even nothing at all, which brings me back
          to mangoes, whose taste like love can be too much,
                    its nutritive flesh sicken,
              its juices dripping over lips and chin,
the way I guess the blood dripped over the hungry lips
          and chin of Odysseus' mother as she lapped from the dish
                    her son set before her in Hades,
              blood that could have been his own,
while the other ghosts flittered about in the twilight, squeaking,
          waiting their turn, and Odysseus waited to
                        find out how he'd get back home.

GHOST IMAGE

My mother enters with two old ladies. "Do you know how
to turn the TV on?" "No," I say, turning on a wildlife program
while sprawling on the armchair. My father walks in,
his young man at his side. "Keep your wings in," he says

and digs me in the ribs. Why can't he just stay away,
puff his big cigars in hell, dig into steaks big as those he'd
seen New York fireman eating in the '30s and envied all his life?
Why can't he just drown again in his own "Cutty Sark"? I go

back to the Galápagos Islands where Darwin is collecting a plant
whose digestive juices work like a man's. He is observing the
start and end of things, how each is trapped, how correlations
are almost numberless, how there are only a few forms and

almost endless variations, which makes me think we are
workings whose laws are left to chance as the screen flutters,
on the blink again, just a flickering ghost image floating in it
and voices fading, which I can't turn off.

THE KNIFE

I found it at the very back of my desk drawer among medals,
dingy ribbons, old coins, dust. On the silver cardboard-box lid,
"W. R. Humphreys & Co. Ltd., Sheffield, England, Pocket Knife,

'Radiant'," and inside reclining calm and beautiful as "Olympia,"
on a coffin of cotton-wool or cloud-bed, twin blades folded
into mother-of-pearl. My father gave it to me, not sure what else

to do with it. Maybe his father gave it him, and his him, ages ago,
all doubtless hard men of few words, and those sharp. It lies pristine,
an illegible date like cuneiform scratched on the back of the box.

I pick it up, the size of a sardine. The longer I look at this
descendant of Mousterian or Clovis the bigger it seems.
I open up a blade, test an edge, draw a bloodline across my palm,

and listen. *"Knife"* it says, the *"k"* sounded, gutteral tenius. I fold it up,
lay it in the box, stick it in the back of the drawer where I hear it
mutter clod, cunt, cretin, krippen, and I try again to forget it's there.

THE DROWNED BOY

I searched into the night, diving down
through the moon at the center of the lake

where weeds floated and there among
the stems my hands touched something

and I pulled it out and headed up
breaking the surface into the moon and

drew the child along backward
on his back and the moon took his face

so there was nothing there but it was still
my face that took everything in and reflected it,

the sky and himself and the lake and me
trying to save what could not be saved.

GRANDFATHER CLOCK

The hour lifts. Rime clips
    the railing like a reliquary
circling, and sleeps. There's
    an albatross' wing wide as the
clouds so you can understand
    sky's limits though you've never
seen an albatross, imagining it as
    a giant seagull, all appetite. The bird
falls, snow takes over. I think I hear
    the beat of oars, or their echo.
I would like to interact with everything,
    retract, strip, and start again. How
impersonal it all is out there,
    a grain in the sky like granite.
A sound in the hall, the grandfather
    clock I've taken with me each time
I've moved though I only had one
    grandfather and him dead
over fifty years. Its chiming
    can be ignored but without it
there'd be nothing for that
    corner. I wind it up each week
hoping it will stop and I can
    clear the corner out, clean it up,
take everything to the dump
    ("Recycling Center"). One large hand
lags a bit, a number or two droops,
    the trunk's big as a bridal chest
with room for a bed of flowers.
    When I lose the key I always
find it again. I've tried not winding.
    It seems to wind itself, calling my bluff.
The minute hand stays still, twitches,
    hesitates, then jumps the gap. I remember
as a child wondering what was
    in that timeless empty space

when my grandfather who one moment
    I was watching in the garden
weeding, the next comes in
    and drops dead at my feet.

98

FOUR IN MEMORY OF RAYMOND G. BROWN

(1)

FLOATING

The old white pine we've cut down still lay head west.
The tarp lay crumpled where he'd dropped it.
Under the trumpet-vine sat a clump of his hair he'd
cut that summer. A plate of ice on the grass resisted rain

and my face swung in the glass sides of the bird-feeder.
In the sleeping loft I found a tin box with faded photos:
him in uniform astride the turret of a Sherman tank, smoking,
a baseball with best wishes from Spud Chandler,

undeveloped negatives of a blonde in profile, and a trick
photo of him and his wife of one year, the cancer in her
even then, rising a quarter-century back over a balcony
of the Empire State, about to float over Manhattan.

(2)

LIGHT

No point in reproaching the dead.
Everyone stays, and comes out of you.

And sometimes there's a way back
to them, even if the path goes in wide loops

past the unweeded garden, past strips
of black cloth stuck through the chicken wire

to keep off the birds, past bare bushes and—
a tree is suddenly flooded with light that

seems to come from nowhere and suffuse
like a flame behind a waterfall before gathering

itself in like the ball of light his mother
as a girl in Russia saw enter the house through

one door and float out through the other.

(3)

THE LAKE

He has come back to walk through the deserted rooms. He smells the shadows,
moves around like melting ice on windows while the room fills with light.
And suddenly he remembers everything: streets of the Bronx, the Grand Concourse,

his Russian mother's teas of grasses and herbs. He calls her name, but she
is very far away, a girl watching ball lightning float in one door and out
the other. Looking out his window he sees birds in a great fan widening

over the Catskills, first one sway, then another, blessing the small brown house
on Ohayo Mountain where someone has come by and swept the floors, polished
mirrors, stood up on its point the cello he could never learn to play. Listen:

water is rolling over cliffs in great shimmering bolts. He watches shadows
of smoke over snow. His eyes move like amazed animals through a world
so suddenly removed until a new sun rises over stone walls. He rises too

and walks among them. Landscapes reflect off his skin. The sun lengthens.
From way off here, you can see a man, now little more than a fatherless boy,
step out into the center of an unmarked lake.

(4)

IDENTITY

They wouldn't let me identify the body. When his two
nephews came downstate the city morgue was closed.
For a week they shuttled up and down, never arriving

on time. So the body just lay there until they phoned to say
they'd seen it, but couldn't be sure. "What do you mean,
not sure?" I said. "Well, he was, well, we don't want to go

out on a limb." He lay there another week until they named him,
alone as when he'd died in his East Tenth walkup railroad flat,
top floor, under a thin asphalt roof that bubbled in summer

and in winter, more than once, collapsed. After Thanksgiving,
when neighbors complained of the stench, the super called
the cops who found him slumped over his desk. "The cats

were going wild," he said. "You wouldn't have recognized him.
I knew him as a tall white man not a short black man.
They had to peel his face off the wood."

THE WAVES

"Where's the past? It's here or nowhere,"
— Italo Calvino, *Invisible Cities*

"Awake I dream..."
— Hannah Green, *The Dead of the House*

We level out and all's well. I reach for the "Times" stuffed into
the seat-pocket and flip through, stopping at an article on his
"blockbuster" retrospective at the Venice Biennale, with a photo
and him remarking of the huge sign "emblazoned" with JACK

WESLEY, "That is really something, isn't it?" Where has he been?
Where have I been? I sleep, and then we are over the water at La Guardia.
I fold the paper to take with me, remembering where I put Jack's cartoon
he gave me for *The Very Last Fish*, and am about to stand up when

I realize I've taken off my pants. Is this really happening? Waves
are lapping at my ankles and I'm with him and Hannah after our drive
south to visit one of her Columbia students near Livorno arriving late,
and the four of us dashing to the empty beach, shedding our clothes

and heading into the dark sea and Hannah, bountiful Hannah,
laughing over the surge, is letting go of Jack's hand, then turning
to beckon me further in, but I'm holding back, afraid of what I cannot see,
what might be hidden under the waves that do not frighten her.

In memoriam Hannah Green (1927-1996)

GHOST DANCE

In memoriam Anthony Burgess

The times are delightful, but always fated
to be long ago, like a pitcher of roses, and
    shadows are lovely, lovely in themselves as essence,
hence this perfect fragrance in the air today,
    perhaps cherry blossom since in Japan, I'm told,
the character for heaven is Fuji reflected in a pool, calm and still,
    quiet unchanging perfection, which makes me wonder
what the character for life is and how you get it
    to stay still long enough to write down, and what
it means when you fix it, and I remember asking
    my old friend Anthony Burgess, now shadow and
reflection himself, "What do you mean?" when he said,
    "Don't do that!" as I spun about stomping hundreds
of roaches that spilled from weeks of unwashed stuff
    in the dishwasher I'd opened to get a clean cup
for the "mother-in-law tea" he'd just brewed,
    black and bitter but fragrant with Bushmills
from a case an admirer sent. "That's life!" he roared.
    But I couldn't stop hopping about to shake them off.
"D'you know," I panted, not quite changing the subject,
    "You have the same English name as Wovoka,
the Paiute Prophet, founder of the Ghost Dance?"
    One hand holding his cup, the other in the air,
a shadow on the wall, beating *contra punctum,*
    he slowly joined the dance.

STRANGE FLOWERS

In a wheelchair a little old lady who's slid
from straight forgetting to flinging food against walls
   to pinching the nurse who was trying to kill her,
"filthy Russian bastard," till she bled, to pinching
   punching and scratching anyone who came near,
"I want to scratch everyone," to singing "The Star-
   Spangled Banner" over and over, she who never sang,
to just sitting and shrinking, flat eyes staring at me,
   she who divided the world into fools and bastards
and I'm still not sure which I am in eyes alien as those
   of Grays who do unspeakable things to you in
flying saucers, now and then taking Ensure through
   a straw the way a weevil sucks sap, sometimes
moving her hands over her face to dislodge the webs
   or maybe she wants to speak so I move closer, but she's
looking, a flicker, a mayfly's wing, past me to her
   daughter's face as if she wants to land there, and her
wishing-puff of white hair stirs in a breeze through
   the window open a crack a bee slips through, and I recall
something about bees remembering a human face if
   they are tricked into thinking we are strange flowers.

LONGINUS ON THE BOWERY

"All memories are echoes"
                        – Grace Schulman

While Grace "hunched in a corner seat" watching Auden with his
Selected Poems on her lap and storing up for "Notes from the Underground:
W. H. Auden on the Lexington Avenue IRT," I could have been

on St. Mark's Place, going to work and glancing up at the plaque
that said he'd lived there, joking to myself "What a place to live,
half way up a wall," and thinking he and I must have crossed paths

many times but I never saw him, unlike Ginsberg who I saw all over the place,
last time through the window of his favorite Chinese restaurant
on the corner of 13th and 1st, razed just after his death for the still

unfinished apartment house I pass each day often humming in my head
like today when it was "The splendor falls on castle walls" and remembering
at seventeen working in Heffer's Bookshop in Petty Cury, both places

long since razed, and that summer selling Benjamin Britten and Peter Pears
copies of Tennyson and Wordsworth, and a year or so later deciding
I was at least partly responsible for the haunting "Serenade," and

as I continued on down 1st I began to remember how I sold Vaughan Williams
a copy of Housman, later to credit myself for his lovely setting of
"Is My Team Ploughing" (and the rejoinder "No, it isn't"), and while

whistling it through my teeth, ignoring glances of passers-by, recalling
how I'd sold Thomas Tallis the original copy, since lost, of whatever text
he used to compose "Spem in alium," that marvelous forty part motet

to transport me for ever when, in college, I sang in one of the eight
small choirs scattered throughout King's Chapel, and, after turning right
onto St. Mark's, glancing up at number 77, walking on until turning

left toward the Bowery I heard Longinus say the soul is filled
with exultation and delight as if it had given birth to the very thing
it had heard, and then I thought up poets to have them say memory

is the moth's feathery antennae that snags and absorbs bits of air's
brightness, turning it echoic in the weave, dilating specters, navigating
a resonance in no need of originals, creation's holy place. It's all on you.

THE RILL

The mountain is a pattern that
whirls, its brightness the absence
   of absence. Walking here is not easy.
Once in, there seems no end. It's
   dark, but some light's saved in
melting snow along the stream
   where a water ouzel runs and
vanishes. Underwater, he looks
   like something burning in a high
bright window. The wind weaves
   back to its source and out again,
going past me past the old growth
   of huge pine the clear-cut forgot
past patches of dark past cracked
   and broken things and back into
those things so they seem whole,
   cues and slews like thought itself
of which this is the thought, the way
   the rill contains itself, overrunning
slabs and rearing back, its clamor
   in the quiet an expression of that quiet,
its clarity what it lives on and gives rise to,
   allowing itself to be anonymous
whatever we call it, faster and faster,
   its freedom restraint, always ahead of itself
in the forefront of falling and falling
   over, moving forward in place.
I follow its pulses that deny themselves
   the higher and deeper I trek, finally
leaving me alone in the center
   of where there is no center.

THE FEATHER

This blue feather from the nest should be a light to see by
        as I turn it around and read off azure, lapis,
lazulite, linarite, tourmaline, sapphire, and
        so on, but each word and angle's undone by the next
so nothing sticks, telling me nothing except
        that loveliness is trapped and refracted for me
to play with, altering with my look, and I'm
        drawn in to where there are no directions,
no frames, just articulation that seems endless,
        even excessive, vivid hunger generated
by emptiness, where color's just abundance
        of broken light, catching, snagging, slipping,
a shaking of the morning star by the wind that
        opens the sky again to blue that is no color
but an idea that limits space and gives us cover.

MAKING IT BACK

I left when a rose flush
on the snow started
the whole thing again and
didn't turn back till,
moonlit, I was walking
through a sub-zero night,
the world's frequencies low
as I stopped to listen,
then followed some moon-
deepened marks like braille
going in and through me but
I was lost, soon reduced to
prayers even if they were
only notes to the self.
Snow on bushes collapsed
as I pushed through. Bones,
bones, and more bleached
bones, trees. I tried to
push ahead of myself to
prove I was going forward
even if I didn't know
if forward was the right
direction, remembering that
in some of the cultures that
were wiped out round here
the past was in front and
the future behind, but hoping
I could come out the other
side by sheer persistence,
along coordinates of guesswork.

MAKING IT OUT

All over these mountains are huge stone walls, piled up
By men with oxen, tackle, crowbars and brute will.
Trees grow right through them, and they still stand.
If you hike these thick woods you'll find them,
They come in at all angles, out of nowhere, cross
And re-cross, holding whole hillsides up, following
Some sort of logic, giving you something to go by.
But try following and likely as not you're lost,
Or if you look round and say *Where am I?* it could mean
You've been here before, and that can mean, after all
That travail, you're back where you started and you'll
Have to pull yourself together again and set off, faster,
In a different direction, beside and over other walls,
Hoping to make it out before nightfall.

STRANGENESS

"Trees, it is your own strangeness…"
– "Trees," Ted Hughes

One of the twin maples that rooted over a century ago in our stone wall,
"line tree," the locals call them, is down. It was always there for me,
cows and horses, birds too, but in its fall took with it part of the wall
and the top strand of barbed wire. The horses are nowhere to be seen

and the cows don't seem to notice. There are other shade trees, even
the remaining twin, and, if they wanted they could make like Bailey,
the adventurous heifer who followed the deer over the wall and into
our woods. But no. As dusk falls to the music of metal ear-tags, they follow

their leader at a fair clip back down to the barn. That tree had been leaning
too far out for years, its main branch twice as thick as a man's waist,
the inside rotted out to duff for my garden, just waiting for a storm
big enough to shake the roots in the shallow soil. And now I'm looking

at it from different angles from either side of the wall, even walking on it,
trying to put things in perspective, take it all in. Parts are still green, and
at the top gooseberry bushes are growing in a crotch. Parts are dust, parts
the planks of a sailing ship with scars like the suckers of a giant squid.

There's so much going on, it's bigger than just "tree," or me, and yet it's
not quite "here" or "there," it's somehow absent or elsewhere. How to get it
straight? How to ask the right questions so it doesn't all come out as if it has
no mind to call its own, as if there are no other minds, as if it's all my fault?

THE HORSES

As I reach across I'm
taller than the backs
I stroke before they'll move
away for as good a reason
as they stayed, down
the steep hill that's
their meadow of thin grass,
more thyme and rock
than grass, brambles and
this stone wall I'm standing on
that for a while keeps us
all together, I and these horses
so large they'll leave behind
their silhouettes as mountains,
where now as I stroke their
huge heads and necks like pillars,
gentle muzzles and soft mouths,
they stand so still under the great maple
that I can hear them breathe
and I talk to them as if they
could understand more than
I can, as if they don't know
that what I'm saying to them
has no other purpose than
to keep then with me and
me with them here until
I have to turn carefully
around on these loose stones,
step down and find my way
back through the darkening woods.

THE CRICKET

A raw sun, just
what it is, scrapes
the last few stars
off the sill. Smoke
and dust drift up but
I open the window wider and–
Listen: something is
cutting us off. Something
is chasing away our lives.
Then out of the gray
a cricket arrives that looks
put together from spare parts.
It sits on the sill beside
the iron lamp and starts
to tune up, a few harsh notes,
and then music as if he
cared a lot, or not at all.

HOW I UNDERSTAND ETERNITY

Organisms evolved colors before
    there were eyes to see them.
I take a look before floating
    to the Cretaceous where colors
are now butterflies and beetles
    shaping themselves to flowers
of sassafras and magnolia. Their
    scents fill my mind while night
starts to warp round me and a
    rabbit in the doorway pauses
by a half-eaten apple. I watch
    the lamplight's clear pool
on the ancient pinewood planks
    fall through cracks and knotholes
onto the lives of mice as starlight
    filters through the window
and falls on me.

MAGDALENIAN

This land's pulse
is silence, an ecstasy
drawing me out and
up to this wide mountain
pasture where I stand
still as the stone
wall while five deer
drawn with quick
clear strokes cross
under the horizon
as if they'd just
stepped off a
Magdalenian wall
into a sketch of
scattered boulders
and hardhack on
hooves sharp as the
scents they release
from thin grass and
dry thyme, before
melting back into
the silence that
shaped them.

MASKS

Tracks make the invisible present.
A mountain wears trees. The trees

wear sky. The sky wears clouds
so we can see how it moves.

The wind is plumed, bringing
three deer into the clearing to drink.

They are cobalt. They are silk
of the stream bubbling through

ice-arches. They are not deer
any more than the sparrow-size

owls who fly about at evening
are owls. They are souls. They are

still full of light so you think
you can see them.

CETUS

We who are used to daily things
are not used to this, whales

glistening as light falls across them,
silencing itself. They do not seem

to move as we stand in the sun's
monotone, the late hour hammering

itself flat while a locust signals
faintly and a finch goes off

in small arpeggios. Even after
the whales have gone we still

stand there, and they reappear falling
through the universe as the sea

sways shut, and a lost bee lands
on my arm, twitching its gold thighs.

IMAGES

Thrush music drifts in so rich I can't quite follow
its bent and fractured notes, the bent fractured, the fractured
bent, quick liquid rills, trills unpredictable, impeccably phrased,
precise yet impossible to remember, sung or whistled, but
recognized each time even with his new trial tweaks and bubbles
and yet nigh impossible to know where the song is, a trick
among trees so you hardly catch a glimpse and even then
it seems to come from someplace else, thrown so the notes
drift to me here, lying in bed at dusk, watching lines
float across my closed eyes, trying to see what's there,
those drifting chevrons, noiseless noteless staves, magnesium
crenellations, glass crescendoes unpredictable as flying saucers
that never land, so clear and almost geometric I feel I could
draw them in detail, the way the Ghent Altarpiece portrayed
an organ so clearly a working model was made from it, but
what I see could not work. What I watch is sleight of eye,
a punch line without a joke, a vigil for a ghost's shadow,
the body of an echo that's the echo itself, pain without
sensation, shape with no body, movement a kind of stasis,
darkness with no dark, the soundless song, the weakening eye
that sees something maybe meant for someone else, not me.

CRICKET

In late fall a
cricket is sitting on
a stone beside an

empty iron lamp, its
chirps bent out of
shape the way sky

can be. It looks
like something made
of spare parts for

an object that doesn't
exist, hoping it all
adds up to more

than just a cricket
tuning itself, scraping
out a few harsh

notes into the dark,
sitting on a stone beside
the empty lamp.

TIME

God didn't create the world;
he is still imagining it between dreams.
Therefore the world is perfect,

if confused, for in it time lives like
spun glass, shadows we live by,
but here it's also a mouth on which

I'll paint lips, where the wind is
generous as a river on which I'll drift
downstream past armies rotting in the mud,

past priests selling heaven, past charlatans
and celebrities, where I'll float over drowned
towns and give morning a voice that rises

and flows around rocks like figures in smoke,
threads of improvisations making day timeless.

THE HOUSE

I follow dark figures moving off under dimming
star routes until in the distance I see a house much like
the one I live in but compounded of light, almost

too bright to see. Holding my breath, I go in until
it all opens up to a space where a gnat singing as
it rises could be the first thing or the last thing left.

I stoop to pick up an apple where there are no apple trees
and feel a wing brush me where I know there are
no angels, until I see one draped in shining shadows,

hear bird song, rare as orchids, and behind it sense
the horizon piling up, the world fresh and anonymous
again, waiting to say its names, while trout flash by

my feet as if a magus had just freed them from
their bodies to turn and twist so where they begin
they end and ending begin as music among bolts of

currents quick as a thought of a thought whose song
arrives the way each star comes home when we call, and
planets float through the windows, little clicks of light.

THE STAIRS

I'm staring at Anna Netrebko on page five,
eyes closed, earrings falling to shoulders her

black hair cascades over. I can hear her voice
as I watch rain burning holes in snow, and see,

floating over the slush, me at my first singing
and dance lesson, the music at odds with my

movements, the teacher pushing me closer to
my partner so, touching her body, inhaling her

scent, I stumble, almost faint, break away, rush
from the room and out the door into the snow, and

here I am staring at a newspaper beside picture frames
with nothing in them. Last night, coyotes sang outside

my bedroom window. This morning I woke with one
in bed beside me and snuggled up to her hips. The carpenter

is coming today to fix the stairs. They don't need fixing.
They go nowhere, and keep on going.

THE HUMMINGBIRD

Snow is falling with no more substance
than a hunch. I wake to moonlight

drifting across my face. It smells
like spun glass. It smells like time itself,

so now it is fall beside the pool near
the house where she died climbing

the stairs and on the calm black surface
I can trace the first stars until I see a

hummingbird on the flagstones near
my feet, and bend to pick up but a breath

blows her onto the dark water so the stars
shiver, break up, and are gone.

– in memoriam, ESM

HRAFN

"Fljúga hvergan dag/ jörmungrund yfir..."
   – "Grímnismál"

Before day breaks
he's already a shadow

on the snow, clipping
the porch, breaking

bits off, smashing
fences, setting off

dogs. All day he
scavenges, scats, and

night falling takes
chunks out of any

light left, wings
fanning fires of

stars he swallows
down to their pulse

so they shine through
him and he's done, off

and flying. What's left
isn't worth having.

THE UNDERWORLD

Going down past rags and bones,
past frost and roots, past
shark teeth, auricles of aurochs,
past teeth of shark and megalodon,
through shells of murex, triton,
whelk, down among the soul's
lattices and ladders, purple sluices
and bones white as daisies, among
corpuscles among clouds of
plankton and protozoa, winds that
move trees like stags, gales whipping
across fens, rain pounding like blood
over steamy greenhouses with morphos
and satyrines, toads and ganglia
strung like lianas, leaves big as huts,
languages of clicks and tongues
liquid as heartbeats, songs of stems
and mud, grubs and microbes,
crystals and dung, and a pulse
strumming trellices of ribs, pulling
it all together where is neither
night nor day, where fingers
move in blind voluptuousness,
naked as earthworms, touching
notes from everything, here where
mind leaves fresh prints on archives,
whispers tracks onto slabs and
bedrock to bloom again and again,
here where is emptiness, the way
a shrine is important for what's
not there, here where music is
the noise silence makes, here where
a head washes up, wave-scoured,
resonant as an empty conch shell,
singing of the underworld.

FAITH SEQUENCE

> *"I speak to you with silence like a cloud or tree."*
> – Czeslaw Miłosz

(1) *Just This*

Under the whisper of Pleiades,
under intaglios and buds of blown glass

I walked until dawn brought
flowers, little bursts of intensity, monuments

to the dark's retreating edge
water is falling over with the weight

of glass bending through glass,
shattering itself like time, saying

nothing, just this.

(2) *The Snow*

       builds up, silent inch by silent inch.
You hope it knows when to stop, but if it doesn't

you could imagine a faith springing up to worship it,
white, the absence of color, its sacred color, words

and melodies based on bird-calls, unseen, never-seen
birds, saving by sound alone, a language so pure it seems

echoes, but solid in that it's all of what's not there,
a creed where reflections are the same as substance,

enlightenment everywhere and nowhere, and where
you know where you are, where you've been and where

you're going by holding up a mirror and watching behind,
in front and all around the enveloping episteme of snow.

(3) *In Remaining Light*

Dawn creaks, wind ground-bass. Dawn grows so slow
you could wring light out faster yourself. Clouds float by

on shadows you can't fix and day passes like a wordless song.
Stones stretch, holding their breath, until it's time again

to let go, curl round themselves as the land darkens, heaves up
into mountains purple as gentians, and everything retreats

into itself, becoming what it can still believe in.

(4) *Redemption*

You, so young, what worlds do you think you can redeem from up there?
I ask again as he raises the flag he'd woven so it flaps its blurred hieroglyphics

in blue air supple as if in the throes of a big idea until a sudden downdraft
out of nowhere tears it to pieces, scraps scattering where they fall, blown about,

so maybe I think this time he'll come down, but no, he'll stick to his perch
though I can now see he's wavering like a slow meteor so maybe I can still

tempt him down and out of his skin thin as star-glow even if all I can offer
is the same old glass world to see with or through, or maybe he'll walk again

with me under saturated blue, past a couple of skinny trees whose few flowers
look contrived, past lizard and snake, till halted by loose strands of barbed wire nailed

to bleached posts across which has fallen a dead saguaro over whose outstretched arms
and trunk someone has fitted a blood-stained tattered shirt all the way to the ground.

(5) *The Result*

I would like to know the matter, the result, and I would like to know where the result
goes, or even if there is such a thing for a result has to be accurate or it could keep on
going to who knows where. God himself from a scientific point of view is really no more
than a starting point of view, no small achievement but hardly a result. It's the same with
the famous vision of "a terrible flood" the famous philosopher saw in broad daylight
where all of northern Europe was engulfed in yellow waves and reduced to rubble. This
was in 1913 and it never occurred to him to connect it to the political situation, as if it
was free standing. Instead he interpreted it to mean that he was "menaced by a psychosis,"
and the outbreak of waves came as something of a relief since he was able to decided that
he was going mad and so escaped the burden and responsibility of being a prophet. "God
is an image," he wrote, "an image yet to come," and so capable of being avoided at least
for a while. The medium of God was hysteria, he thought, with attendant spirits. Again,
looking back, we can see that this was no small achievement since each spirit had a life
story and even its own distinctive handwriting. He said that if your spirit is a genius you're
lucky. If not you're screwed and have to start again. Luckily, we now know that you can be
and go anywhere, be in more than one place at a time (a cryptomnesiac particle). You can
be more than one person, each remembering the other, each making the other though this
could result in a prolonged self-torment as a bodied disembodied spirit, incompatible,
maybe, but not opposites, speaking a private language anyone can learn to speak . It is lit-
erature. It is about God though he is an outrageous fellow, continually disturbing, contin-
ually asking and being asked "What's the matter?" Indeed, what *is* the matter? I search for
something in my life to make this true, all this, or come true, in order for it to be a result.
But I still have no idea where the result goes.

ST. FRANCIS AND THE FLIES

It is good to stay in the window watching mountains,
waiting. It is good to be seated by the fire built
but not lit. It is good to hear the burglar alarm

go off and think Who's there? as I note flies collect
at the corners of high panes, die and fall on me
beside Bellini's *St. Francis*, his state amicable

with donkey and crane and all God's creation where
everything's in place while he stands in front of
his writing desk outside his ramada, gazing up at the sun

or singing the Canticle he'd just composed, or even maybe
looking out for flies in case they land in his inkwell,
clog his pen, or squat on his paper so they force him

to go against his nature and take a page from the yet unborn
St. Bernard who exorcised a swarm of demon flies so
they dropped dead at his holy words and had to be

shoveled out of the church in heaps. But me, I wouldn't
do that. I've trained myself to like flies. If you can like flies
you can like anything, for flies are unavoidable as death,

and as they die are replaced as if they were all one fly ever
since being psychopomps, minions of the god of Ekron,
Baal-zebub, leading souls from rotting flesh to purer incarnation,

and now it's night and I'm at my desk, who knows who it is
circling my goose-neck, or doing a breakdance on my book,
swimming in my tea, hiding in my hair? I could ask, the way

I once asked my cat if he was my dead grandfather and who
gave signs in the affirmative. So, as one fly lands here and
looks about, after I've lightly blown off the paper a leg or two,

a head, and a few wings, the way God's breath, *ruach*,
moved over the face of the waters, I reach for my pen.
Each fly has a story. I wait to take it down.

BEAUTY

I sing here in the mountains, trapped in my house wide
as night, under sharp stars, a light on, two, the fire burning,
snow up to the windows, supporting myself on air the
ice-storm left, no one for miles, and even if they could hear

who would recognize my idiosyncratic repertoire that climaxes
with "Vilja," the soprano aria I can never manage so I put on
the vinyl and Hilde Gueden makes me cry, so I have her sing it
again, and again, a song I've loved since my teens when the beauty

of the world was the beauty of a woman's voice, its swell and
diapason, and the closest I came to flesh was Eustacia Vye's
"pagan eyes, full of nocturnal mystery." A romantic lad,
I ever liked Hitler a bit when I found out that his favorite

composer after Wagner was Lehar, and I almost felt sorry for
Mussolini when I read that "Vilja" could have been the last music
he ever heard when, in Lago di Garda, the morning of April 17,
1945, Il Duce said goodbye to his eighteen year-old son who

was playing the original score of "The Merry Widow" on the piano.
"Ciao, Romano," he said, "keep playing," before giving a Fascist
salute and getting into the waiting car. Eleven days later he was
hanging by his heels in an Esso station. And keep playing he did,

later founding his own group, "The Romano Mussolini All-Stars."
"Such beauty," I think, rapt, gazing out the dark window as Hilde's
voice dies away, until I come to, startled by a large branch
snapping off loud as a gun-blast, and a night bird's scream.

THE WHALE

The village sits on my desk, a hole
in the middle as if hit by a star guided
to the spot. Wires hang. Out of nowhere

a moth comes and squats on the church.
I squeeze into the house on the corner
with the cardboard roof, feed the wood-stove.

The fire flares as the world darkens and
closes in. I think: I can't go on like this,
just as I remember the whale I once saw

whose back broke through then, with a
slow heave, shoved the sea aside and
went back down head-first, leaving

little evidence he was ever there, falling,
for all I knew, for ever into the blackness,
driven by a heart big as a car, its great

song traveling all over the boundless world
which another somewhere some time
will hear and respond to, maybe for ever.

JOY

Here where I stand in our mountain pasture, the wind
whistling under rocks, twisting like a dervish
round sculpted trees, these deep shadows remind me

of those in Egypt where Flaubert wrote and loved the sun
and the bronze dancer stripped to the rebecs
of blindfolded musicians, twisting like a dervish

round sculpted trees and lightly-anchored bushes,
here where I'm watching a turkey-buzzard banking up
a thermal into a steep turn of sky's path, stalling,

righting himself, taking in scents clear as guiding stars,
earth's fragrant smokes rising like delight, until
he's lost in all that sky, leaving me to startled cows

as I step out into the sun, eyes shut, and find myself
free, leaping about arms beating, shirt flapping, flying,
yes, flying wordless to the wind's wild rebec.

VEGA

On my bed in late afternoon I am listening
to the thrush with his song now down perfect
if not pat, and a note drawn across a tractor a mile
or more away, yes, here among scents of honeysuckle
and full-bore blackberry, wisps of bedstraw, just me, solo,
looking up at the spider crossing the ceiling constellation
then out the window where a chipmunk clucks
and a mink is running along the stone wall into
the woods, yes, here is where I would go, no need
to knock a hole in the wall to let my soul out,
the window is open so it can drift off over the beanflowers
and squash blossoms, over the worm sliding back
down after the shower, over the slug determined
to get somewhere, over chickadees in the massive
white pine, the bear digging out ants from a rotten stump,
over the turkey vultures riding the thermals into Lyra
and coyotes who bring night to life, yes, here,
in Vega, today just a general store fallen in and
boarded up, occupied for now by a young woman
who washes herself and her baby in the stream
and hides like a nymph or faun when I pass by.

A UNIVERSE

This morning I thought my armchair was on fire. It wasn't.
Just sunlight like an intense companion. And when I went out
later everything was still burning, slicing through the razzle

of butterflies, over clattering sparrows, baking the terrapin like
an amulet into clay, shaping the heron who stabs through
his reflection and flies off with what he's got, the leaping flash,

sunlight making the snake a gem, wrist-thick, whipping across
the path, a flick, a curl like the Pueblo sign for flowing water—
there! skin like foil, a flare through wind slicing the red maple

and nudging the chipmunk mining the compost, finally ending up
on me filling my basket in the garden before the sun shatters
on night's shield and sheets of moiré flow in shaking out stars,

green, white, gold moidores clicking on night's throat,
cirrus of pearl spinning with the sound of crumpled cellophane,
swooping, centering nowhere in a laughing Lucretian universe.

MOUSE IN THE HOUSE

Now stiff is how I rise and how retire–
no, I don't mean that, I mean "stiff,"
as in board, and no, this is no joke, as
Dr. Lee notes, pointing to a place on the spine
he holds up which reminds me of those I saw
dangling bloody in the souks of Algiers, and
I get so absorbed I don't hear what he says,
and the pain doesn't help either, but
I thank him and try to remember what
he'd said as I walk out the door, though "walk"
is hardly the word as I move carrying my spine
gingerly while it creaks and clicks like our
old floorboards and stairs, or whatever is
gnawing through our walls, a mouse, I guess,
though at times it sounds like a hyena crunching
bones. I want to catch him before he gets to
the wiring and the place burns down, as happened
to one of my friends, but he must be as supple as
a hurdler, leaping all the traps I'd set from
basement to attic, or negotiating them like a
sapper in a minefield, though sometimes he sets
one off and scarpers with the peanut butter,
flowing like lymph into the house whose insides
he knows better than I, and sometimes when
I don't hear from him for a day or two I think
he's gone, finally taken my hints, but then,
as I sit mindfully on my sticky mat, wondering
what the MRI will find when the last one
came up empty, I think I hear him starting up
again in joist and beam, bracing, rafter, wall.

SONG OF THE SCYTHE

Sharpened the scythe, stroked the snathe's
rock maple curved like a spine, balanced
the grips and–down go the daisies, down
the crown vetch, clover, grass high as
a house until the thin point snags on
matted leaves, digs into a clod, bounces
out of my hands that held too tight–
don't grab, keep the heel down, step
and swing, step and swing, hold light if you
don't want to amputate a foot or lose a leg,
sweep round, go with the flow from the hips,
let the swing and sway move you on as steel
peened with hammer and jig makes its
definitive sound, the cut and crunch there's
no gainsaying or second guessing, it's final,
and the grass falls down easy and tight in swathes,
sweet hay–take a break now and then to hone
the blade with the whetstone you keep
in your belt, sound of sea on shingle, so again
the curve's a sharp frozen wave and in my head
I can't stop dancing as I look around at
goldenrod and ryegrass, wake of small saplings,
wild oats, speargrass, huckleberry bushes
that had worked their way back in, and it's
hard not to get carried away by the sway
and sweep so down go more vines and fences,
telephone poles, car, house with the shape of the gesture,
joy carrying me along as if I had an appetite
for everything and could go on for ever, things
falling into place before, behind, around,
my eyes closed, letting the scythe sing
its song, its song, on, and on.

FROM OQUAGA

They're having fun, my neighbors,
I could curse them but this is
their life, this land is their land
on which they pursue happiness
with weedwackers, earthmovers,
buzz-saws, ATVs doing wheelies
and devouring streambeds, shotguns
echoing an invasion, coke cans
strung up and peppered full
of holes, and beyond that cars
and trucks, back and front hoes,
CATS and hammer-rigs and–
ah, a pause. Lunch, perhaps, so
now if I'm quiet and the ringing
in my ears subsides I can hear
the wind's brute history shaking
gold from trees, this old wind
blowing right at me from
down the road, from Oquaga
again with the smell of burning
lodges and the sweet smell of
scorched flesh and through
the smoke the screams of children
we've caught in the October corn
and have impaled on bayonets,
"holding them up to see how
they would twist and turn," and
their screams fill the air,
like birds in the wind.

BILLETS FOR BULLETS

Ever since they moved in it's guns all day
                and half the night.
            Rifles, shotguns, assault rifles,
whatever. But sitting at my desk, like now,
                is worst, waiting
        for the other jack-boot to drop, shaking
the house like a thunderclap directly over-
                head—just now
        my heart stopped, really stopped, and I
almost fell from my chair—oh, that duo who,
                when not firing
        guns, strap on weed-wackers or hop
astride a mower, a cross between a Sherman
                tank and a
        Maserati to chase down every
weed or blade of grass until they corner it,
                then, as reward,
        slip into a rubber dinghy
and race around the pond picking off frogs
                and whatever else
        is cowering in the reeds. But silence,
as I said, is worse, since then you don't know
                what they're up to,
        and think perhaps they've driven their truck
into town to freshen up their ammo
                stockpile. Big
        mistake. For if your nerves begin
retreating into place, your heart fall back
                into its slot,
        the blood begin to flow again
between pollarded banks, and the creative spirit
                gets ready to find
        its nock, then—they've got you! *Wham!*
Bam! Wham! And there is nothing to be done.
            They're within their rights,
        the sheriff says. Get used to it.

I look across the valley to the confederate flag
                    fluttering halfway
          up the slope where the guys have decided
quiet is the better part of valor
                    and only shatter
          it when they blow up Saturdays,
or Sundays. But these two have no political
                    axe to grind–
          God forbid they should get their hands
on axes. I'd move if I could, but where to? Back
                    to the silence of
          the city? No, I'll keep on hoping,
hope the real way since hope isn't hope "until
                    all ground for hope
          has vanished," and try to finish my work
before a bullet strays across the red
                    dirt road and finds
          its billet, a phrase taught me by
my grandpa who still carried a bullet in
                    his chest "from Wipers"
          and kept another the size of a finger
in the gas-mask hung up in the shed, and ssh!,
                    I hear a bird
          outside my window, its song reminding
me of the one I heard as a kid in the Newcastle
                    department store
          where you put a penny in a slot
and the bird on its perch in the cage began to sing
                    for as long as the penny
          lasted. It knew when to stop. But this one
seems stuck. If ever I could corner the market in silence
                    I'd give it away
          for free.

THE BIRD FLYING HIM

Pigeons burbling with tails outspread, a woodpecker
bending his beak banging away at an airconditioning unit
ten storeys up, mayflower and locust giving off pheromones
and whiffs of estrogen on this first day like summer
after a winter of digging out. There is no reason not
to include them while I postpone the pleasure
of cleaning my fingernails with a sharp penknife,
though who uses pens today, after a night of scratching
and poking, trying to make amends and be forgiven in a plane
skimming rooftops, about to crash, wanting the slate clean,
because things can't wait, and it is good to plan a better future
this Earth Day e.g. up giant redwoods older than Parthenon
or Pantheon whose canopies sprout huckleberry bushes
and even other trees, who can reverse the flow of water
if they choose to put out fires in the underbrush
or back up in their heads when they catch fire.
In this other world lightning's the norm like jolts of caffeine
which you rush to catch before it completes itself or
passes away like the long poem I wrote in my head
without words to make it new about the framers
of the Constitution based on a review of a book
in the *Sunday Times* but for the life of me when I
went back to check details it wasn't there, just books
on indie rock and reproductive rights and the like,
nowhere to be found among the "stunning tours de force"
and the like. Maybe it's hiding under the one
poetry review of a poet long dead, but no. I look
under and there's only "Major Acquisitions" on top of
Tibet and coming-of-age novels. But you can't waste
more time looking in the loam. The tree might fall,
huckleberries and all, leaves swaying in collapse, roots
neither wide nor deep. You have to push on or
fall off, swimming down at ninety mph, lungs flattening
into the small space we come from, back into our own
bloodshot eyes, the trunk becoming stone columns, fluted
to mimic origins, the wood we came from, the blood

reversed into mosaics, gold tiles, birds and deer always
representing something else, and, wings tattered, we land
in a hole, a cave, Etruscan maybe, a spring still burbling
in the prison floor like San Pietro in Carcere that held Jugurtha,
Vercingetorix and even St. Peter, it all almost caves in on top
of Michelangelo who next door takes a hammer and smashes
the knee of Moses so what could have been we'll never know
since all that's left is Leah and Rachel, the composition
for ever incomplete but complete in another way, lovely
broken scales flowing in and out, up and down and through,
like clouds of starlings Etruscan augers read from, making
another music from down among the dead to up into ecstasy,
shaping, cleaning, cutting and still I can't find that review
of the book on the Constitution which would pull everything together.
Maybe I kept turning the page with another struck to it
with sticky dirty fingers on hands that need more washing
the more you use them and whose nails gather mortality
I need to dig out. Or it's just not there except in my need
to have it there, my need to know how things became the way
they are and what we can do to improve them before the sap
reverses like the tide and sweeps all away, goes back
underground leaking into the dark from roots surprisingly
shallow. Maybe I could have imagined the whole thing
or it was there once for a while and never again
and is now in my mind where somehow I have the book's
synopsis and argument which I remember in fragments
because I got excited and started planning a long poem
on an important subject which would be reviewed in
the *Times* and make it to the best-seller list along with
Dan Brown, Mary Higgins Clark and Danielle Steel.
It starts in hexameters with the Constitutional Convention
on the hot summer of 1787, hot as today, hotter maybe, with
Franklin pointing to the carving of a sun on the back
of Washington's chair and saying he doesn't know
whether it's rising or setting. The whole business was
a bit of a mess, and a wonder at the same time.
It could have gone many ways. It could, for instance,
have been hijacked by Rutledge, and it certainly
ended up cobbled together with slavery and no Bill of Rights,
shored against its ruin by later additions which I'd have

to ignore as it grew and balanced, its idealism the result
of rough bargaining by "demigods" and "coxcombs."
But then I got sidetracked by pigeons and woodpeckers
and all the rest until, flipping through a book on the Lost Colony,
I found de Bry's engravings of White's drawings, and stopped
at what White called "The Flyer" and de Bry "The Coniuerer,"
a man in a fur loincloth with a tasselled pouch, and a bird
flying in his hair, flying him along past invisibility.

DAME EDNA, JUDY TENUTA AND JOHN ASHBERY

I am on a journey to somewhere, but bought a ticket for a station
further on. I read a while, then put down his *Selected* on the seat
next to me, and "As I sit looking out of a window" at a bit of this,

a bit of that, I watch the cozy shift of the world until I close my eyes.
Bumping along, on the back of my eyelids pictographs play on clouds,
and a collaged landscape keeps knocking into itself while trying

to avoid expectations. We've been going quite a while but we're not
even anywhere near where I thought we were going, or where
I thought we had been, so I try to hum to the train's smooth irregular beat

to pass the time. There's no schedule to keep to, though I keep some sort
of time rocking from side to side in the gently disconcerted shift
of the world and go into a deeper sleep as if breathing in oracular wisps,

a kid again, my head under a towel over boiling water in which my mother's
dissolved Friar's Balsam, inhaling deeply to clear conduits and tubes
and learn to breathe again, when my wife, still suffering from a nasty cold

and listening to Nora Jones, calls out "Hey, wake up, listen to this:
'Dame Edna has volunteered to adopt Anna Nicole Smith's daughter,
but only if she can rename her Lois. *I once had a baby called Lois,*

she said in Sydney. *It was stolen. It didn't get much publicity. I was out
and when I got back there were horrible koala tracks, giant koala prints,
and we've been looking for her ever since'.*" "Do you believe that?"

I ask. "Anything's possible," my wife sniffs, putting the newspaper
down on the seat beside her, blowing her nose and turning off Nora Jones.
"It could happen. Do you remember Judy Tenuta?" Do I? I love her.

CANCELLED

I watch large drops hit the swallowtails, sending shudders
through their whole bodies, knocking them off maple leaves or
out of the air, and recall my father telling how he battled Nazis,

luring them into clouds, then began to gnaw another hole
in the hospital blanket, and my mother sitting at my kitchen table.
"You're not half the man your father was," she says,

not looking up from copying more aphorisms and proverbs
into the already large collection she lived by, where
each one somewhere cancelled another out.

HERO

The war over, he flew in on the feathered glory of RAF wings
stuck to his chest, and a box of medals on which was written
"What a hero. What a weight." He carried all before him, even

chasing his mother-in-law waving something she could only
describe to me years later in shocked euphemism. He bought
a second-hand MG which worked when needed, but when

his uniform didn't, he dumped it into his wardrobe along with
cartons of black-market Winstons and Lucky Strikes. From time
to time he'd take it out, squeeze into it and try his luck again

with the ladies. No go. He tried to make a go of all sorts of jobs,
but the heroes who'd stayed and manned the home front had
copped all the decent ones, so on a dark night he flew away,

and was never heard from again, leaving his togs at the bottom
of the wardrobe along with brittle packets of condoms, a box
of medals, magazines and cigarettes that wouldn't light, being stale,

old and damp. Years later I found him in my bedroom mirror.
You might think I'd say "Let him out. He's been in long enough.
At least grant him parole." But I don't. So there he sits in a child-size

chair bolted to the floor. I'm sorry, he mimes through the glass.
Innocent. "Oh, sure, innocent," I mouth back. We're in this together,
he replies. To myself I say: Live with it, and turn away.

FENLAND VIGNETTES

I: *Mail at Xmas*

The war a dozen years over, my father who fought the Nazis bravely
(though the Germans were "our brothers") has been warning me again

that the commies are coming for everything including his second-hand
Morris Minor that barely fits into his garage and once in seldom leaves.

They're welcome, I think as I pedal the red GPO bike with my heavy leather
GPO satchel through this greasy orange street light morning fog spreads

over semi-detached houses, whose house numbers are indecipherable until
you go right up and stick your nose on them at the new housing estate called

King's Hedges Road, where there are no kings, except the three I bring, and
any hedges are buried with ancient Angles in rotten fen sedge and gray mud

under rime-encrusted postage-stamp lawns, here where I wander round and round
on my heavy bike, lost, banging into things, bearing tidings of comfort and joy.

II: *Digging Come Spring*

Heavy gray marl sticks to my spade, water seeping into the deep gash I gouge through
rotten sedge and reeds, sucking at my feet, the old fen rising in a line we pile near where

they'd built another council estate and found an Angle burial ground. In this stink of
ancient air I stand up straight to breathe. "Kill it, kiddo! Kill it!" laughs Shay, one of the

Irish navvy twins, shoulders too wide to fit into the trench, posing with one foot on the pipes
we're laying while rolling giant clay phalloi, balls to match, which he demonstrates for

housewives who watch from behind curtains, colored scarves round their heads, pretending
to look past us across their small dug-up lawns into the distance and its bit of sun.

THE HEROIC

Here where land was dug from swamp and sea, balloons rise,
silent annunciations going the wrong way. Someone shouts
from a hole in the sky. Rain falls. When night falls
it brings dim stars and a slit moon, and I find myself
thinking of Rembrandt's one-eyed Batavian king
with his band of grungy revolutionaries swearing
a sword-oath, of those who go against the grain,
tell the truth and pay the price, the old master
cutting up his masterpiece the city fathers rejected,
leaving only a fragment to torment us. All care
about heroes, the self-possession, the rage like rocks
between the teeth, so why as I cross canals tame
and acidulous do I see rise in the dark California,
where I've never been, lemons ripening, long gardens
where mulberries hang and air's elastic, where you
can say to yourself there are so many ways to be
happy and monumental at the same time, where girls
dive into waves like seabirds and come up somewhere
out of sight, forever anonymous, untroubled, young?

CONTINUO

Albinoni's Adagio in G minor for strings and organ continuo,
a line of washing waves in the morning breeze from Ostia as a
girl-child moves slowly down a circular staircase from the roof
into the half of the courtyard still in shadow, Albinoni, a palazzo by a canal,
arabesques over the water gate, a merchant's sign over voluted windows,
a dromedary with a large load, and almost lost in rain sweeping in
from the Laguna Morta the sounds of carpentry, some comfort in the scent
of wood and sawdust, and in the hill-fort near the chalk-pit where we
gathered fossils they found in a corn-drying pit a sack still
secured by a single bronze needle and inside that a girl about six,
legs severed and head missing, and in a rubbish pit a woman
about forty with crushed pelvis, lying beside the burnt bones of a horse,
and when I was five Lancasters and B17s dropped hell on Dresden
where now a replica Baroque skyline is rising so time is unhinged
and history never happened, and while I watch a mink with a chipmunk
limp in its jaws runs across the road where the week before
I'd seen a catamount they say no longer exists here just as they said
the wolf I'd watched in the woods behind my house was extinct,
while the Victor's cockpit had dug itself into a corn field
after the crash with the Canberra, bits of both scattered everywhere.
A holly tree had burned but not much corn. No survivors. It all looked posed
as I drove through the Devil's Dike from the Wash, just after the Russians
invaded Czechoslovakia, and the TV said now they will have lost
the confidence of the Afroasian bloc, just as I did when not long ago
I found out that Albinoni's Adagio in G minor for strings and organ continuo
which I'd loved and counted on was written by Remo Giazotto in the fifties,
but at least the lovely "Dresden Amen" that had haunted my skull since
choirboy days now had something like its old home back in the reconstituted
Frauenkirche whose model had been Venice's Santa Maria della Salute
where as I tried to pray I had my wallet lifted and my watch slipped
off my wrist. "Ah Ah Ah Aaah-men."

NARRATIVES

> *"Narratives are one sort of trace we leave on the world"*
> – Gary Snyder

"Stand in front. Here, hold my bag." She reaches
    under her skirt. Digs a hole
with her heel in the gravel of the taurobolium.
Buries it. "Joining all the blood down here,"
    she says.
        Upstairs, on the way out,
  she rinses her fingers in the basin by San Clemente's
great doors. "They were all over the city," I say.
    "Churches were built over them."
"Tertullian says Mithras was invented
by the Devil to mock Christ." "More like
    the other way round." "That's history for you.
One big *puticolo*."
        By the time we get
to the Largo Argentina for a 64 bus
    the sun is overhead. Where Caesar
was stabbed in Temple C a cat is licking himself.
"Do you think that's where we get the word 'understand'?"
    she says. "You stood–" "Not you. Men only."
"You stood-under the grill and the blood of the stabbed bull
poured over you and you under-stood. Immediate,
    unmediated transformation.
No blood of the lamb there." "It's certainly something
you'd remember." "All I remember from
    last night is too much Frascati, three
  young nuns dancing, and we were in love." "Still are."
The bus comes at us like a chariot out of the sun.
    On board I say, "Remember Rtis
in the chariot leaning down and saying to Mithras:
'Step up closer. Bend down'?" "I do." "And as he does so
    his loose Mede trousers ride up. Rtis embraces him
  and says, 'You have such handsome calves'." "They marry."
It's the wrong bus but somehow we still arrive
    at the Vatican. "It says here St. Peter's
was built over a cave." "Mithras," I say.

"He was everywhere." "This place is too big and too much.
        It tries too hard." "Somebody said
    it would make a great bronchitis hospital for those
with delicate lungs and delicate fantasies."
        "I prefer the solar bull to the pale
    Galilean," she says. "The world has grown gray from
his breath."
                We get another wrong bus and walk
back home through the Campo de'Fiori. She
        pats the base of Giordano Bruno's
    statue, where he burned.
                        That night, on our balcony
in the ghetto, we stand looking up over the city's
        lights at the sky's coronal loops, the power
    of each part of sunlight. "All those stories
in the sky. Who's your favorite?" she asks. "You mean
        the magnetic field of the sun's fusion,
    the pure force of the Milky Way, the inner
necessities of the Virgo Clusters? Do you know
        that 'myth' and 'mouth' are related?"
    I say. "It makes sense," she says, "but I'm
not sure I like your latest story." "It's not mine.
        And it's not really a story. It's science."
    "How can you tell science it's got nice calves?" "You can't.
And who would want to anyway? There'd be
        no point. It wouldn't understand."

DA VOLPINI

We're worming our way into the fifteenth century
                grotto-cavern under
the house where St. Ignatius Loyola lived.
"Just one glass" begins the ritual as Volpini
                starts to slide open the
huge door a bit and blinks. "Just a taste.
                Then you must go. I'm c-
closed. What if the p-police find out?" We
squeeze in to find the cobbler, an ex-bandit from
                Sicily, walking around
with his brother, whispering. They nod, then
                leave. "Brolio?"
    "Why not?" Volpini vanishes, returning
with a bottle, and his stutter, more a stiff
                crick of sound in
his throat that lands on the lips of terracotta
                oil-jars under
a wall plaque for his grandfather from
the College of Vintners signed by the Pope in 1856,
                as light from one 50-
watt bulb gleams off the bald pate
                of the seventy year-old
virgin where Pope Pius X had patted
his boy's locks after a nun had swatted them. He
                holds the bottle up to
his eyes and stares, enthralled by the mold
                on top of the cork. He
sets it down, takes his penknife out,
cuts round the top as if making a graft, takes
                a corkscrew, works
it slowly in, pulls it gently out
                just to loosen, moves
the cork side to side with his fingers until
it just slips out. "Mmm," he says. "Just look at it.
                The cork is pu-u-urple. Beautiful.

58. Smell. Mmmm." He pours it into
                beakers and hands them round,
          refusing one himself because he says
he has to go to supper at his sister's, although
                he knows we know he's
not, that he'll sit here till midnight counting
                his money, dipping his fingers
into the water on the saucer beside the Chianti
flask on the marble-top table. But slowly he
                relents and says he'll have
          a *ditto*, so I put a long finger alongside
                a glass and pour as he
protests. We know what comes next. He shuffles off
into the dark and returns with a tin which he opens
                slowly to reveal
          bedded on tissue a cigarette Anthony
                Armstrong-Jones gave him
on a visit incognito with Princess
Margaret. "Talking of which," says Edward, "today's
                the *onomastico*
          of St. Edward the Confessor." Yael says
                his name means Michael,
which sends Volpini off for a calendar which
he riffles through confusing the Michaels, the saint of the angels
                with the archangel, while
telling us the story of the Roman fisherman
from the ghetto here who caught a huge fish which
                Ottavia, wife of the
          emperor, saw from the palace window which
                site is now occupied–
he starts to draw in floor-dust when *Knock! Knock!*
Enter two polizei, one in blue, the other in
                green who wish us all
          good evening as Volpini hands them
                two glasses and pours while
the one from Pompeii extols the virtues of
Vesuvian wine and the Tuscan says his wines can't
                be beat. "It's the soil,"
he says. "Sun," says the other. Volpini
                says it's Eduardo's

saint's day and they toast him. "Auguri! Auguri!"
As they leave they tell us to drop by their barracks
              for a glass. Volpini
    says now we must go, but we want to discuss the
              virtues of Vernaccia.
    "Mmmm," he says, and goes for a bottle
which he holds against the bulb. "Ver-er-naccia," he whispers,
              and from the label reads
    "Aiuta il lavoro p-psichico e
              le rea-realizzazione
artistiche..." I buy it, the Sardinian
green-gold, 700 lire, and set it down
              later to toast on
    my own the principessa from Bologna
              the three of us had
    stayed with several days, sleeping in
the same bed until she threw two out and kept
              me to tell her story
    to, underground anti-fascist work,
              capture and torture, how
    years later she went mad and in the cinema
everyone moved away from her before she realized
              she'd stuck chicken-parts
    up her cunt and lettuce up her ass,
              so she ran home and
    threw all her dishes out the window till
the police came and she spent a year in a rest home,
              and then I think of
    the exercise mistake a student at the Magistero
              made turning "We stayed
    at that woman's house for several days" into
"That is the house whose woman we stayed in for several days."
              And then we leave, Yael
    still upset about the death of Che,
              who will later leave
    for Sweden, where Mossad will hunt him down,
and, they say, in a case of mistaken identity, kill him,
              and Edward, on the run
    from Nam until his liver caught up with him,
and me, "lurking disembodied in this memory grotto."

SLUGS

I prayed for rain and rain it did.
The moon brought the rain but
the rain brought slugs. I did not pray
for slugs. My neighbors say the rain

makes slugs the way rotting meat
makes *mosche*. What use are they?
"The law cannot be known properly
by thought and discrimination," says

the Lotus Sutra. So I try again. Looking
close, they seem relaxed and easy-
going in shades of orange, brown, gray,
some striped, some fat as my thumb.

They can give you a nasty bite, my
neighbors say. They've bitten you?
I ask. Not yet, they say, and piss on them
until they shrivel up. But I try to see them

in a different way, pebbles in a Zen garden,
helping attain no-mind, non-attachment,
no judgement. Now even the word
"pebble" makes me feel better about them.

So I try working with Shiko's koan of the earth-
worm he cut in half while hoeing and asks
which half has life but it turns out somehow
to be about the hoe, which could be the

creative mind. In any case I keep on trying
on behalf of slugs which is, of course, on
my own behalf since I do not wish to know
the world like Audubon by stopping it. But

no one has a good word to say about slugs,
and as I watch them heading out in
morning's cool to bring my Eden down,
"plant, fern, and flow'r," I try recalling

the bestiarists who found a use for them.
But I soon quit and, taking a page
from my neighbors' book, making due
allowance for wind velocity, gauging parallax

and allowing for vectors, arcs and angles,
taking careful aim,

WORLD'S SHADOW

On my adobe's red-earth floor something is making the light jump
like a jack-rabbit, up and off whitewashed walls. The flowers outside
take in canvas or run it out, stretching their brightness to morning's
indigo which they breathe in and turn glassine, and I think: things are

only so deep, emblems of rhythms not the rhythms themselves, hints
to pick and twist to other dimensions the way those buzzards are rising
out of sight in wide baldacchinos following air's grains, while round them
gray skeins draw down and across to form the sky-loom the Tewa say

the world is woven on. The rain is still in distant mountains as the sun
breaks free and tries to stand alone, then begins to move toward me,
drawing cloud-threads into a lovely tree that flickers and unfurls.
It's a trick, I know, as I watch it spread into a huge bole and branches

draped with Spanish moss, but hanging from a bough by his neck is
a black man, a doll in the photo I found as a child, a marionette that still
stays on that tree twisting, an ornament bloody and unsexed, as worshipers
look up smiling, posing for the camera, men women and children my age

at their world's renewal, so I close my eyes, trying to trace the lovely tree
climbing from the earth over sage and creosote bush, up into the world
of faded star-bones, into the icy vastness whose shadow this world is.

AT TLALOCAN WITH YMA SUMAC

From my window more windows, more frames,
    no blue, just glass, cordoned, confined, and reflections
    of blue and sometimes white or gray, and when night comes
it makes everything night, sucking up any color and turning it
    splotchy, yellowish, in patches, to go with the black that keeps
    building up and slipping off in flakes like skin, and behind
the glass people watch TV's unearthly light and dream. Or not,
    or do things, or not, like working out on a treadmill
    that doesn't really work and jerks along, and stops, though
why I imagine a treadmill I don't know. Maybe I should have them
    doing yoga, except nobody round here does yoga unless maybe it's
    Octavio Paz, and he's dead, or unless it's because I write
fast with a pencil that goes where it feels like and treadmill means
    something special to it, like this famous Swiss writer I read about
    who used "the pencil method," its rhythmic flow, the rhythm
of reverie, the "unique bliss" that calms you down and
    cheers you up, slipping over the page's white ice,
    cutting figures you had no idea you knew or even knew
were there, and that's how they found him after he'd
    gone insane, frozen in a field, cutting his own figure
    on his back, sprawled in the snow, all he had to
fall back on, eyes wide open as if still trying to see,
    mouth agape, as if still forming a phrase, though the hand
    that held the pencil was a claw, like Big Foot's at Wounded Knee,
his world gone with him forever, taken, never to return,
    the world where everybody talked, animal, tree, stone, us,
    as easily as the way birds slip through air, expand and link the air,
make it thin enough to move through, thick enough to glide on,
    where you can see further and further even when you know
    so little and can say even less with hands stiff from rheumatism
and a right metatarsal thick from gout, punishment for gluttony,
    double comic because I eat little. I wonder: when
    you're reborn from this place are the hands healed
and is the big toe and the other parts reborn like a baby's,
    cool and placid as the swans that swim like clear ideas on the lake?
    "Can anything satisfying be found on earth?" sang the prince

Nezahualcoyotl, which sounds a bit petty for one who had it all.
     "Wait it out, señor," said the doctor when I told him I couldn't pay.
     "This too will pass." Pretty good advice, I suppose, that fits
about anything, one way or the other, even here in Tlalocan in the rain
     where the buses from the springs of Chapultepec and all points beyond,
     red, black, white, blue, pull up and let out the various
drowning victims, those with legs and ankles swollen with dropsy,
     fellow hobblers with gout and those lightning struck down
     on mountainside and golf course. If you photographed this place
in the valley, aside from the willows and waterbirds, the accustomed
     and conventional green corn, squash, sprigs of amaranth, green chiles,
     tomatoes, string beans, flowers and quetzal plumes, you'd get
a foamy effect, like detergent, a glittering like fishscales, a flickering
     like fireflies on water thick and opaque as isinglass. And if the camera
     could run backwards to before I even got here it might also show me
planning at least in my mind to train eagles to hunt iguanas
     in the Sierra Madre after I'd counted on the draft to be a hook
     to snag on, catch me falling, except the board made me 4F, or later
after the one review of my only novel to date, the one that said
     my characters (which I'd carefully drawn from life) were like
     fairy-tale creatures whose world had ended and who couldn't cope
with "the real world." "Real world!" But it might also catch me
     arriving here because I'd heard that the wondrous liquid
     Yma Sumac was from these parts and I wanted to get to know her
in her natural habitat. It turned out, however, that she was either
     an Incan princess, as she said, or Amy Camus from the Bronx,
     as the papers said. And in any case, she wasn't from hereabouts
and I haven't met her, yet.

OFF THE PAN-AMERICAN HIGHWAY

I can still see myself looking up at Shirley Jackson's widow's walk
    in Bennington & thinking how thin the modern veneer
    even though it was only a story & though it takes more
of an effort nowadays to imagine the mind behind the knife
    that gave to Tlaloc the baby born with a cowlick, &
    even if we understood, what then? The priests were
virtuous men. And I was being virtuous & civic minded when
    I made a compost pile at the bottom of a tall tree
    in the park of derelicts & druggies since it would later
help feed them from my garden, especially since the tree
    was protected by padding almost to the top, like an
    Aztec warrior. But when I went to the town hall to ask
them to keep an eye on it they said nothing could be done.
    So I just had to watch as kids piled up tires &
    old mattresses & wood so it looked like a
Guy Fawkes bonfire & when the garbage men arrived
    they picked up some & set the rest on fire,
    rich compost & all, the stench woke me up with
a terrible hangover in the hotel room of a town I'd
    arrived at by chance pulling off the Pan-American
    Highway at nightfall & thinking it was somehow all
my fault they'd hung up by their feet those three thieves,
    strung them up like Mussolini from that big tree
    with white blossoms, gagging them first, then beating them
like piñatas so bad the blossoms were red, & castrated them
    & set them ablaze, still alive & squirming like hooked fish,
    while the fiesta continued all night & the smell of burning wood
& flesh hung over the dancers, mingling with festive smells,
    & women danced with women, mothers with daughters,
    aunts with nieces, grandmothers with granddaughters,
each in a full white dress over petticoats & lace, white
    blouses embroidered with flowers like a garden, gold
    jewelry, all beautiful & looking like Frida Kahlo & as I
walked around that morning nobody could tell me
    what the fiesta was all about or why it was called "Vigil"
    unless it was because no one slept & who could sleep

on such a night & nobody knew anything about three thieves
    so I thought maybe I'd had too much wine & had read
    "The Lottery" one too many times, until I came to the plaza
& a scorched tree, dark splotches on the grass, & as I walked
    about, other trees, & patches where no grass grew.

THE STAR HUSBANDS

The night sky was so sharp & insistent I forgot
       I was here or anywhere.
    This is what I'd worship, this
"resurrection of presences," this is what
       I'd want to keep going,
     by blood if necessary, rather
than the pure brute fact of the sun. I tried
       to call them off the
    lamp-lit verandah, to come out,
it was something seldom seen from these
       volcanic slopes so often
     misty, the sky filled with water
droplets, smoke or dust. But they kept talking,
       bits reaching me–"... and they
    used to say *los indios no
oigan por las nalgas*...and..." I try
       again. "I've seen it before,"
    called out Lucinda, "near Montreal"–
a jab. She'd known my ex. But why my need
       to share? Proof, like counting
    coup? Proof you exist under
so much vacancy? So I stood beside
       the jacarandas & broken
     lemon trees looking up
& didn't feel lonely, thinking that to them
       up there I too could be
    a spark in a dark firmament,
& again I called, asking them to douse
       the lights, if only for
    a moment, & come out with me here,
but they didn't hear & so I walked further
       into the dark looking
     up & falling about, the mind
emptying, punctured words escaping–*shack,
     knife, clone, rope-a-dope,*
      & more, stars ringing, stuttering, clicking

in place, moving about, settling down
          into lines, whorls, shapes with no
        narratives, in an unknown syntax but
singing with light, & I lay on the tired soil
          that once uttered sugar's sweetness
        & as I lay remembered the story
of the two young Indian girls who lay down on
          their backs on a night such as this,
        looking up at the stars deciding
which they'd like to marry until two handsome
          youths arrived & carried them
        off way away where it was too late
for them to change their minds & in the version
          I recalled they never returned.

LOST IN TRANSLATION

They're talking of Pedro, the name, the rock on which
    a church was built based on a pun, and how mistranslation
    gives us "virgins" in the Muslim paradise instead of "sweet raisins,"

And how "young woman" becomes "virgin" and another
    religion is born, and how a lost translation of buried
    gold tablets produces those young men in gray flannels,

White shirts and knotted ties who come out to save us
    even on hot days enough to melt water, save us
    from rooms like this where the sweet smoke is locked in

And passed around and where I open the window
    onto the street. My visitors this evening include mole-eyed
    middle-aged lawyers from Valle de Bravo whose kids are

Fresas, strawberries, who do lines on 10-lire bills and go
    "to the desert" for the divine flesh of mushrooms.
    Flower scrolls flow from their mouths, the intoxicating

Flowers that could be morning-glory, *ololiuqui*, the same seeds
    kids in college chewed and then flew off the roof past my window
    and onto the grassy courtyard and the emergency room.

The light goes out and night is set in motion
    as a marquetry casket. I hear music, the entanglements
    of insects, the dark opening onto a place where

The desert cools. "There is the courage to exaggerate,"
    says Angela. "Why does the body confine itself to truth,
    or clothes?" One day, I say, I will take all you say into consideration.

But then I will leave like the Franciscan down the hill to seek
    even more deprivations and humility. Angela says she's
    an artist and tells the story, again, of Courbet in the

Sainte-Pélagie Prison painting Paris from the top floor the way
        he painted his seas, as if everything was the movement of waves.
        So, I say, he saw everything the same way. How useful is that?

Streets are no sea. They suck you up. "To heaven?" she says. I say
        there's a confusion of genres here. I will call this *song*,
        so there's nothing to prove. "Do you know the story about the reed mat?"

Says "Conejo," the English teacher. "The coiled snake, the live deer
        and the bird hatching eggs? It's all about power. Or," he adds,
        "the story of the Pope aiming his blowgun from the Place of Willows,

At the roseate flowers and butterflies shining like the wind, the jade wind
        blowing through cacao flowers?" "Nope," I say, "but I have just read
        about the Chief of the Federal Police who used to live in Culiacan and who

Was killed after he arrested Osiel Cárdenas of the Gulf Cartel." "They own
        us all," says "Conejo." "The chief was my uncle." Then he adds, "meth
        is easy to make." I thought he said "myth" and was about to disagree

When a pick-up shot by, AFI officers in black, machine guns, flak jackets.
        "They just wait till they leave," says Angel. "And then they come back out."
        They're heading north where the city has dried itself up. I can see them

In the Chichimec desert, among dust, arroyos and rocks, everything suspended
        in its own time, becoming light that goes in spirals, moving about
        not touching the ground, fragrant in its own way, turning into more

Of what it is, melting the way we're told a fish in fear of its life turns into water.

from COMPANIONS, ANALOGIES

DE SENECTUTE or BEST YOU CAN

I have nothing more to go on, not even
    that–a half of something, a half-life, less
and something else, and wonder if this would
    be enough for another life, in another life,
and if what was had the compatibility to
    suck on time, suck in time, help me live
in it if only in the way of my recurrent
    nightmare of still living in the house I sold
years ago, prowling about, anxious, on the alert,
    like the priest at Nemi, until time continued
with the silent crush of whatever it's made of
    that from a distance looks like a still flower,
red and white, or just white, or red, coming
    at you balancing on "itself," which is what
I'll call what it's in, something like a brilliant
    hummingbird flying forward backwards so
fast you can't see it, or a bubble balanced on
    a meniscus so you can't see it but it makes you
think of what comes next in another time when
    nothing does, so how do you talk about something
like eternity without using grammar which is
    shape, sequence, number, without needing
a mask to pull on believing you can pretend
    you exist even if somewhere else since once
you'd put it on you've lost sight of it and don't
    know who it says you're supposed to be and
have no basis for action, or otherwise, and could
    do anything and nothing could be proved against
you, then as you leave everything behind and have
    no idea what all this would be in another life
or lives let alone this, when we live on without
    knowing, perhaps next to, in front, behind, on top,
beneath everything and nothing, and whatever is
    between everything else, the way we don't look
at just one thing but relations between ourselves
    and things, which means what we see is always

floating in the gaps where you can be united
    with "yourself" or whatever you go by now, or
with what you've got left to judge with and which
    you hope enough to get on, best you can.

HEADING OUT

Behind curtains drawn across back lanes, in the parlor kept for show, a couch,
untouched harmonium, curiosity cabinet, a fire when switched on just shadows

on a screen, caged bird a penny played. Here a boy, standing on the cushions,
reaches past the gold-leaf frame, through a forest of giant trees to slide his fingers

down the only beam of light to a dark pool where on a rock a naked man looks up,
head back, mouth open, calling the way a stone might, his voice rising to the boy

the way waves rise, shaking off the cries of gulls while across the parlor wall
five ceramic ducks fly in formation, each smaller than the one in front, heading

through the window and out across the lane, across continents, to where they
don't know, or when there won't know if they're there, or here, or somewhere else.

QUANTUM FOR BREAKFAST

You're sitting at the table, which they used to say was empty, but now
the table's waking too, flying about opening hallways and entryways, corridors
and staircases, whole families crammed into what used to be porticoes, camped
under campaniles, stuck under stones, under aqueducts, and if they choose

their particles can fly about at breakneck speed like hummingbirds in
Teotihuacan or pass through someone sitting on a barstool in Trastevere,
or even you about to jump off a roof holding pillows in front while wondering
if fractals have fractals and if so how long and how far and how many worlds

are there and for how long, for as Alcmaeon said aeons ago, man dies because
he cannot join his end to his beginning, and some other sage said there are worlds
extending in every direction, visible and invisible, and we do not live in this
little moment but in that world extending in every direction, and Plato himself

said mind resides in seeing affinities simultaneously, and Ibnul Arabi that there is
no such thing as time, and someone else claimed that the non-existence of the world
was never in time, so I sit half-asleep with this still in my head waiting for what's
in store from a world not what it is, waiting for what it might be.

MORE

Last night in a dream I traced the edges of leaves,
stems and blossoms with a Micron 02 pen on top

of a sheet like Plexiglass which hadn't yet
been invented. Pressing hard on a top flat and secure as

a sheet of paper, I concentrated to get each curl and
edge right, before standing back to admire my work.

That was when I noticed more to it than surface. Lifting
the box against the light, plants glowed inside, fixed

at the height of their growing season, floating immutable
as if in ether, in more than four directions. I tried to get

closer, inside without opening, catch each niche and
nuance, fleck and fragrance, trace it on itself without

changing a thing but making it mine, or at least more
than itself, more than me, more than its finale.

WHO OF SHADOW

Shadows have shadows. Sometimes
that's all they are, all the way down.

They broaden you out, tighten you up,
can run as fast, stay as still, move

without you, without moving you.
When you look down you can trace

their nothing but can't see them
sideways. They refigure light

as dark but won't break down,
just drift away, adjust to what

you still can't get, you who breathe
shadows elusive as owls:

*Who? Who? Who do you think
you are?*

THE LEAST OF IT

We lose nothing by not knowing since
everything is ours and we give it away
freely. It may fit perfectly, but now it's

too late I want it back, this is not a one-
way street or mirror, you can't wear me
like a hat, one size does not fit all though

I still plead for you to make room, the way
the moon does or, presumably, the sun
though it's too far away to know for sure,

and I am at the point of my life when I
realize we are not trees, never were, nor birds
or mountains, not anything we can't be,

the unseen is still the unseen, or if it's
seen is meaningless as shadows, for what
might have been no longer is and that

leaves us with very little, just deserts and
formulae for more of what we already are
but no plans for anything else, or more, which

is what we really need, and now it's too late
to be as we reach for fire that won't burn but
with no way to hold it or put it out once it's

eaten our hands, the pool and all the genes now
gutted, just this side of nothing, everything
flapping, and that, as I said, is the least of it.

FIRE WITH FIRE

overwhelming, wings catching, a taste for everything, hammers
striking sparks, reaching, its flowers roar and spit scattering scraps—oh, there, how
the hawk tilts over and away, loses itself as I hide and peer through the conflagration

taller than trees it takes out to see roads petering away where the twister hit, lightning
caught and way off burned-out sky in its poverty, its ashen aftermath, until the wheel
turns to night I breathe over the lake now clear with new heavens, smoke-wisps

cooled to unearthly lights, flickering liquid all round me in flames, swimming sky-water,
water-sky, bird entering unknown shapes and shadows, nebulous, how glorious
in amorphous echoes of skeins and flares that flutter around me viridian, amethyst,

streaks roseate and mauve, watered saffron and shot silk filtering air while an owl calls,
coyotes sing, dip and quiver, night winds calling soft flames, new fire staining my skin
as I float on my back, sky flowing through my fingers, in my mouth.

BECOMING

The beat of oars, precise footprints neat as shadows over
the surface of the void, moving together, race along the course

with no room for the approximate, leaving a trail to follow
the way letters began as the mark of cranes, messages in the blue,

and where to go forward you look back at the irreversible,
the consequence, chaining you to it, its tight whorls moving over

the surface, so it's as if you stay and they move, telling a story
in which you can't see where you're going until you've been there,

become what you are and betray at your peril.

AT THE OPERA

"die Scenerie war Abschied"
     – Rilke, *"The Fourth Elegy"*

If you look out to sea, you see what the sea wants,
but here it is painted backdrop behind the sailing ship
on wheels that's pulled along on ropes behind the balustrade
till it has to stop and disappear as marionettes, moving
with jerky emotions, sing their farewell duet, the sea
unmoving, waves' skin stretched and gleaming over
an invisible shoal. But we will cut the sea some slack,
puppets too, who are doing as well as can be expected,
and as for the music, it is almost too big to hear as it
evokes absence, opens up loneliness for which there
can be no preparation since it always comes on its
own terms, even via dolls. So I close my eyes. Too late.
The seas have risen, a gale in the rigging is tearing the
sheets apart, snapping ropes and stays, until a wave
washes the crew overboard, wrecks the ship on the shoal.
The curtain falls. The sea rolls up. Puppets crumble.
Who's there?

FALLING

As the stream suddenly spills from quarried-
out heights, rises and snags on itself, chokes

in spray, balanced in its back flow, freighted
with rocks, stones, trees, star-shards, crushing

itself with its own weight, a leaf caught in
an updraft is tossed about, falling but steadied

by its own shape, free as it falls so as I watch
I say it is almost not falling at all, it is hardly

a leaf as it opens a space for itself, tracing
emptiness etching itself on air.

TO BE TREE

"O hoher Baum im ohr!"
— Rilke, *Die Sonette an Orpheus*

I stand inside the white pine, braced against the trunk,
head a bird, hands needles, sometimes an hour or what
you call time when you can't count, ignored by what
or whatever, a planting, a co-tree, its consciousness

in human form, an inflected self hoping to become
what it is or feels itself to be but not to think of what it is,
just the last chance to turn away, back to where we once were,
fragrant, green, head a longing realized somewhere else,

all sense, a love focused, not to be a tree but not oneself,
no antecedent, no purpose, but desire that lay in wait until
it grew a tree to be in, looking out as a branch to touch air,
the world mediated as wind, leaving you as you were

but not the same, here where you can't lie down so
look up through the branches, here where you stand
in perspective, the height you need to know, so you
stand still and listen to the silence in silence and this

you've come to hear, the hollow rich reverberations
all around where nothing happens, where the world opens
out to itself so you can go on for ever, where there's
a tree surrounded by other trees but this is the tree

you want, the one you stand in as in a flame, and you
flare within it, no one would know the difference,
if they saw anything at all they would just see a tree,
they wouldn't see you, they wouldn't even look twice.

PROOF

After rain I walk down the path, looking about, roots
and rocks, birds, staring into the trees, probing. But
"looking," Plato's highest sense, still doesn't give me

proof and I feel a bit like his Lydian shepherd who
could see everything at a distance and was touched by
nothing, so decide again to give a chance to Aristotle who

said "touch knows difference," and am about to go touch
trees, trace leaves, stick fingers into bark I might even
lick and bite, the way a dog or baby takes in the world,

when I think that perhaps Plato was right, touch is of
the senses lowest, a "mediating membrane," but then
remember how the Buddha, challenged by Mara to reveal

his authority, simply bent over and touched the ground,
which I'm about to do when the scent of damp earth
floods my senses, and there's nothing to prove.

SUNDAY OUT OF NOWHERE

The clock on the church tower is so simple
its difficulties come from elsewhere, from
curving the dial inward with a broken arm
to bumpy bits in air, even loose bells. No matter
how well-meaning God may be he is still God
and destined to the absolute which means we are
pretty much left on our own so the ordinary even
unpleasant past from a distance looks loved
only because it is complete and if it was going
to hurt us it already has and we are still here.
The clock pulses as if it were a facet of language,
syllable by syllable, building, so when we say
"it pulses," that's what it does, though it does
another thing which could be expressed another
way or not at all, as if we wanted it to mean more,
the way when something pressed to the wall pushes
back, broadening the base of its being, and ours
as we respond, respecting it, figuring out like me
what's what and what isn't, for the seasons change
fast as I look out over a playground now an ice-rink,
over lopped London plane trees to the power-station
that exploded in the last storm surge when seawater
reached a giant boiler and I thought we would all die
as it all ticks down pretending it is just the clicks
and chirps of sparrows, a drip drip, and all Sunday,
out of nowhere I found myself weeping so I couldn't
turn back, waiting for something while strangling
myself with the phone cord trying to get on as if there's
anything to get on with, like one of those trees, just
doing it, the clock banging on, or be a place where
you can be your own guest so there's no need to be
polite and you can tell the truth and even say Fuck Off
without giving offense, you who are fucking off.

NIGHT

"...to find a form that accommodates the mess..."
         – Beckett

Windows fallen away, you can't tell
where you or anything ends or begins, edges
folded in, no middle, so to hold you spread
into yourself where what's to go on, the
room gone, a flat shot of itself, dimensionless,
no portents, no gifts, you're stuck with each
piece not even itself, not even the space
between, there is none and you still reach
out with this weight in your chest, incubus
racking your ribs as it would take you
off but you cannot be found, not
even an outline, shadows of a shadow,
but–there, what's left as you move
your hand to trace dark's edges, not
entirely human, entirely human, what
by day you can forget, but not night.

ARS MORIENDI

LEGERDEMAIN

To shine, invisible, the door open
and no one there, to lie a shadow

on the grass, the abstraction of the visible,
watching and not seen, without conviction,

without opinion, disappearing like holding
the breath forever, always the same thing,

no name, the dark object light waves bend
around, to be the light paralysing attention

so it arrives at the eye without exciting
the regard of the soul.

ACROSS GALAXIES

> *"Spooky actions at a distance"*
> – Einstein

I could almost hear it when I listened
and still didn't take it for granted so that's

how it became luminous, coming at me
from way back as if it was lights down

a long alley or an afterimage of the unseen,
a crescendo of distance ticking like clockwork

over blue snow-fields rocking themselves shut
and *Not yet, not quite yet* I would say, parting

syllables as if swimming through to get
to the other side under safer skies always,

despite everything, stone-cold sober to
engineer my way to where opposites lean

in to keep each other up while behind them
float particles that have interacted in the past

then moved apart, but if you can still touch one
its partner dances instantaneously no matter

how far away, even at the other side
of the universe, even across galaxies.

WALL

A chipmunk dives into the old stone wall
I'm on, his home and harbor, taking

what's given, navigating crevices smooth
as air. I love him, the wall's lymph, its

voice–listen! flowing through everything,
calling you to find the ventriloquist so

you follow what you can't, through halls,
down corridors, by hanging gardens, onto

vistas he gives you opening onto new angles.
If souls exist, he's one.

SHE LIES BESIDE ME

To my daughter on the sea-floor, to the way
she married someone unknown to me
and left which was when I let myself know
I was in love with her in an old-fashioned way
just as she was beautiful in an old-fashioned way,
full figure and green like the plaster statue of
the naked reclining woman on the sideboard
when I was a kid, beside the fishbowl with
the goldfish, round and round till I got dizzy,
watched through the bowl, mermaid
quivering in the currents, blinded by the light
through stained glass, yes, my daughter I took
for granted, to the way I saw rare migrating birds
the morning after they crashed into my windows
at night, to the way she told me she was getting
married in Sweden and then I was angry, jealous
as a cat, for he didn't deserve her, whoever he was,
she could do and knew so much, more than I,
and it was now all for someone else so I'd have
to tell her I was in love with her to keep her
for ever but instead I told her smoking was bad
and she had to stop though I knew she wouldn't,
and her marrying someone her own age was a slap
in the face, I might as well be dead as again I watch
her swim naked in the bowl, glorious though inclined
to weight which I hope swimming will keep off
at least for a while until she returns because now
I'm afraid that if I turn around she won't be there,
and why in Sweden? I think, maybe because she
looks like Ingrid Bergman or Anita Ekberg and
I can see her in something like "Smiles of a
Summer Night," though she should watch out
for those meatballs, and why did she leave without
even a note, I didn't even know she'd gone but
I soon found out and followed to a center for spiritual
growth that included sauna and Nordic track and

yoga to discourage ego where things were so arranged
that I was only allowed to watch by looking into
a floor-to-ceiling mirror behind the wooden benches,
sitting with my back to her to discourage intimacy,
watching reflections, which was getting nowhere so I
decided to return home but found I had no money,
just a credit card, and the barman gave me a strange look
as if he thought I'd paid but wasn't sure, and I wasn't
sure myself but pretended I had, and kept drinking, to them all,
Mona and Myra, gorgeous blonde Finns, all of twenty,
you couldn't tell them apart, who took me everywhere
with them, at thirteen surviving my first nocturnal
emissions, awash in love and confusion, confused
with worship and erections, and to Agneta who I
imprinted on a bit later, hair long and thick as
a mermaid's, wondrous breasts she went home with
to Gothenberg one Christmas but returned without,
which I didn't understand but thought had something
to do with over-exercise, and who brought me back
a SKF ball-bearing key-ring. I will always be walking
with them. Where did they go not to grow old?
And now she has come home, my daughter, back to me.
I watch as she sleeps in bed beside me, gold hair
in ripples over the pillow, shining even before dawn,
breath regular, luxurious, Aphrodite of the foamy sheets,
I peeping Pentheus. When she wakes, she will go to
the kitchen, make breakfast, the same each day, for ever.
Today, I will take her to look at the basil just germinated
on the windowsill. I don't ask her what she's thinking
because it is what I think, I know where she will go
and what she will do when she leaves because she is
still with me, and I don't ask where she's been
because I was there too, as I raise my glass to
my daughter, all of hers, all her, all of her.

SKY BURIAL

(Basil Bunting, 1900-1985)

At my beat-up maple writing desk, stuck,
I look out over maples turning red and find myself
remembering sitting with him among roses,
celandines, black and white crystals from a local
coal tip, looking down from Wylam ("place
of the water-wheel,") to the once salmon-crowded
now frothy Tyne, "washing machines," he says
sipping my gift of Red Label from a mug taken
from a bar with no bottles. "Principle?" "Penury."
He moves, groans. "You know, in the Sudan
they put men down at seventy and eat their women
as soon as they become grandmothers. In Tibet
when you die they chop you up and leave you on
a mountain top for vultures, 'sky burial,' so you
end up as vulture dung, your epitaph." As we watched
a train worming its way from one side of England
to the other, a seagull flew over and shat on his shoulder.
"That's good luck," he said, wiping it off with a tuft
of grass and tossing it down the hill. "I've had a
twenty-line poem on my desk five years now waiting
for the last line—and just found it."

THIS HOUSE

When I get to the dining-room and its three fish
trapped in a bowl I take off my boots and go barefoot
into the parlor with its birds in cages singing so loud
I can't hear myself think, so I go to the library where
I can be with Scott of the Antarctic and his son Peter
who, before the war, gave my aunt a signed watercolor
of ducks, some geese, in flight. I'd nailed it to the wall
next to a print of Brice Marden's "The Muses," a frieze
of green, white, green, blue loops evoking a procession
of Zeus's daughters who we follow one way and then
reverse the flow and start again at the other end.
I'm thinking that Memory is the mother of the muses
when a stone crashes through the glass and lands
under the desk. I look through the broken pane at a boy
running off. A bell rings but nothing happens. I light
a cigarette though I don't smoke. I'll change my shirt,
I'll change my shorts. What holds them up? Memory?
I'll change my life. I'll write it down. I look for a note-pad.

NOTE 1: Day-trip

A small steam engine is pulsing at rest in the middle
of the viaduct over the Derwent at Rowland's Gill.
Women are taking off my clothes for a shivering
cousin Neil who has just charged down the bank
and fallen into the river, practicing to be a drunk
on an oil platform in the North Sea where clothes
would be useless when they fished him out and
laid him on the rig where he is now just a memory
of a summer day where one boy falls and another remembers.

LOOKING FOR THE LOST

How what you are stands clearer than the fresh-turned earth
   because there's a death inside us that's more than crooked
sleep though we still want to love the body– how I used
   to love my body, which is to say the sunlight and low angles
of dark and how I fear it now, the way it changes so that hand
   reaching out before my eye is stained and spotted like time itself,
like the memory of time, marsh miasma, someone else's
   simultaneous mummy. I don't understand, so how can I trust it?
And yet this hand and its companions, while not perfect make do
   as a serviceable hybrid that chugs along and bottoms out
from time to time but that's part of it, the life you've known
   though you can't really root for it any more, it has its limits,
it's only there a certain way, if done right, for a short time, so
   when you get a certain age and look back it all looks accident
and yet at the same time inevitable, so you keep working at what
   you don't quite have hoping, when the time comes, it will still
work for you. There's a lot more to it for there are always questions,
   always more hands to reach out and back through the open windows
where the passenger train is itself the scenery we watch from,
   black fields moving on that were rich fens, deep, but now drained
to the price paid of silver coin for haring-silver, segge-silver,
   dust rising east in a wind from the Urals blotting out the track,
the land shrinking and dropping, though still how beautiful,
   shining loam, bright sillions, yet no more islands to reach up
and hold onto so you're left holding your own shoulders in your
   old hands, muscles taut, the land posed like von Hagens'
"Yoga Baby," skin framed in situ, identity "not provided," alive
dead, dead alive, plastinates adding "Pregnant Woman
   with Foetus," carved with the maker's signature, and a room at
the end, "Visitors May Choose Whether or Not to Enter This Room,"
   where we find "The Wonders of Human Development," flute music
piped in. What development? Who should see this? "Anyone interested
   in learning what makes us human." Is it art? Is it science? Is it
a funeral parlor, moving objects constantly multiplying themselves,
   mirrored taxidermy, moving away from oneself into oneself,
so where have we gone? Let us look. There are always questions,

everything incongruous, as if our ambition is to be invisible,
anywhere and everything, alter egos with alter egos, posed and
   invested in attributes, time as anacoluthic, everything at once,
trying to beat it with whatever comes to hand, not philosophy's
   isolation of the concept but a dream of particulars, not so much
ague and hacking cough as pike jack-knife, even a diorama flash
   of teal, neck-dips, distant down-notes, splash and drift of tench,
corncrake's *crax, crax*, bittern's bassoon in reeds, "bumping," the
   speaking marsh new-coined from sounds themselves cast from
air's core, where lilies' lamps shake so shine rings out at wind's
   swipes of alder scattering flower heads, numb in the spinnies,
buckthorn, marsh thistle, crusts of blue flag and a gust tracing across
   itself, across the mere, whiff of cow-tad, turve-fires, fish blood in
barrels, path through the carr petered out in oatgrass until the moon
   opens quicksilver, guilder-rose, a splash where night's full
of rotten harrs, boggles and wandering lights, reason enough for
   some to have drained the place, and as it turns in cuts, sluices,
clows and sasses I marvel here in the Catskills with a boy's wonder
   at the Claud's great driving wheels hauling "The Fenman"
over black fields toward Lynn and look out the window at all this
   and the old fen slodger with terrible catarrh who wandered into
the ER saying his foot "itched," after he stuck a spike through it
   years ago. But when we peeled off the filthy bandages the itch
was maggots, the itch gangrene. Everything had passed him by and
   not much meant. All my life I have looked for the lost, and lost.

NO CIGARS

– for Jack Wesley and Hannah Green

"Great clouds," I say, looking out across the studio
when a breeze blows its yellow scent of broom up
from Cagnes onto a corner of the canvas where sky
will be. "Look at that," says Jack. "Did I tell you
I worked for Boeing? There," he dabs. "You have
to find a way to keep sky up. Clouds do that."
Silence. Jack is mixing paint. I sit remembering
when I brought my father my first book, inscribed
to him, neatly wrapped. He opened it, stared.
"What's this?" he said. "A *book*?" It flew across
the room. "I thought it was a box of cigars."
"Boeing?" I said. "Yes. Flying machines." "My dad
was an engineer. He admired accuracy and precision.
He also loved art. He even copied Manet's 'Déjeuner',"
made the frame and hung it on the wall. When I
found you in one of his art books and told him
you were my friend, that was the only time I ever
impressed him with anything. He even said he would
read my book." "And did he?" "He did not."

WHAT GIVES

Old fruit in my garden bobs on the branch,
    human, stout. Crows fly in and
take it apart, the way ravens took apart
    dead warriors, going first for the eyes.
Over the hill, the tide goes in and out,
    a second theme related to the first.
Sun stuns the birds, it does not let them go.
    It does not let them through, they're *here*.
It is noon, Roman ghost-time though
    this is not Rome where I slept each day
till noon when the wind from Ostia
    came through the broken windows and
woke me up. I dreamed in Rome of Rome.
    Where you are is never where you are...
Clothes on the roof across from me
    billow out and a lovely woman
rearranges them with one hand, the
    other holding down her orange skirt.
Later, she and I will meet and at Veii,
    by tombs, by ancient rock-cut sacred
bathing places, on the terra cotta earth
    that yielded statues of the Vulca School,
among nettles and daisies and buttercups,
    to the sounds of frogs and one cuckoo,
make love... Now there's a line of oranges
    left at the high-tide mark, blood oranges
from crates dumped or washed overboard
    in last night's storm...
                    One thinks of the human,
meaning the dailiness of things, a family's clothes
    on a line, oranges and crates of oranges,
tombs, frogs, cuckoos, the swelling sea,
    women, the wonder of women, the importance
of tomorrow which soon comes due, even here
    in the mountains where each summer evening
I watch the waxwings find their way home

heading west over my house, cheeping
as they fly, always a straggler or two trying
    to catch up and calling louder as the stars
begin to move in, or seem to, as they did
    at Veii, Cerveteri, Tarquinia whose augurs
turned them all, birds and stars, everything
    back or into the human, prognosticating the
true course and nature of things and on tombs
    had painted scenes more vivid than life itself
so what is left behind is not the world
    but some version of what it meant
to be alive, not what is given but what gives.

THE MOON

Despite everything, it's still my birthday, so I whistle and sing silly
songs, old songs, *Here we go loopy-loo... O bella ciao, bella ciao,*
bella ciao, ciao, ciao... I'm happy in the kitchen, throwing together

my rat-tat-touille made with whatever's ripe in the garden,
ennobling it all with handfulls of basil. Vasari lies on the couch,
under Gigli's *Diario Senese.* But books are graves. No books

for me, no recipes either. I'm making it all up as I go along.
They're not my books anyway. They're my wife's. She can read
later. Now it's party time. *Par-tay! Par-tay!* Just us two. *Here,*

put on this funny hat. Try on this squash blossom. Here, hang these
scarlet fagioli from your ears. Look what a big zucchino I've got!
At my age any pleasure's worth having. The body's still built for it,

the way the old chestnut trees were built for the full moon I watched
last night as they let go a bit at a time through gaps of broken branches
so she climbed up above the house, gathering herself to herself,

filling up as if to stay, moving into whatever space stars had left, so
they trailed after her like silver drones over vineyards where wild boars
rooted, over the partisan caves where porcupines gnawed chestnut

trees planted after the war, turning their spines into fireballs while
in the Radda churchyard she illumined the plaque to those
UCCISI DAI BARBARI TEDESCHI.

THE PALERMO ROAD

In memoriam Basil Bunting

Outside Trapani, snow on the mountains,
                    dark red earth,
          terraces, orange trees, cars following our
dust-cloud, we following theirs, others
                    overtaking and
          cutting in. A three-wheeler with a black pig
straining in a net, another with three
                    little girls giggling
          waving and choking on our dirt and fumes,
and Walter still fuming insisting on the daily
                    history lesson
          he's memorized: *Between the mouths*
of the Fiumara Zappulla and Capo D'Orlando
                    was in 1299
          fought a sea-battle in which... He slows
slower to think what comes next and a dignified
                    old man in a
          black suit with black armband overtakes us on
a donkey with wood planks strapped to its sides.
                    In Palermo
          a priest frowns when I ask, but points. We
find it after scrambling over iron railings
                    Judith gets
          hung up on and round walls W gets stuck
between: "Teatrino dei Pupi Armati,
                    Guiseppi Argento
          & Figli, Via del Pappagallo, 10."
We enter an empty barn with whitewashed beams,
                    a few decorations
          for Natale, '67, pictures of the palatins
in armor on the walls. A man motions us
                    to follow him
          backstage and up a steep ladder past
grinning cannibals and Moors. At the top
                    along the walls
          puppets almost life-size, rods to hands

heads and legs, the oldest one, he says,
                    one hundred years,
            we can have for eighty thousand lire.
"Ecco Orlando!" A body with three heads,
                    boy, man,
            old man, surrounded by shiny shields that
took a month to make. Back out front
                    the wooden benches
            fill. Six people at five hundred lire each.
Against a painted backdrop and to music
                    the story of Orlando
            unfolds. You recognize him by his cross-eyed squint,
denoting ferocity. He comes to Charlemagne's court
                    to swipe some soup
            and vitals for his mother and sister hiding
in the rocks. He calls the emperor "Magnomagno,"
                    "Eateat," and
            runs away pursued by two retainers. When they catch
him he smacks them about until his ma
                    recognizes them
            and they go back to beg pardon of the king
who knocks her down and Orlando knocks him down
                    and yells:
            "I'll kick him in the teeth and knock him out!"
Then Charlemagne forgives his sister,
                    embracing her
            too long for Orlando who yells, "Hey, *basta!*
Enough of that! Hey, break it up!" More battle scenes.
                    Swords clash
            on swords and shields above the barrel-organ.
Saracens fall in heaps, and twitch,
                    many with
            their heads lopped off. One runs around
like a chicken with no head. And then
                    the action stops
            while the *puparo* runs from behind the scenes
to sort out boys scuffling with the organ-boy
                    for his job.
            The losers settle down to cigarettes and
hacking coughs. After, Walter's miffed.

                    "Why was there
              no Orlando going mad when Angelica
betrays him? I've read the book. He recovers
                    his lost wits
              by sniffing the urn they're in which Adolfo
brought back from the moon, and which..."
                    "Astolfo," Judith says,
                "not Adolfo." Next day we aim for Cefalù,
W mad because J still refuses to share a room,
                    and still upset
              because at a mosaic of a "*scena erotica*" in
Piazza Armerina of two lovers embracing,
                    she with her back
              towards us, drawing aside her gown to show
her arse, he said he saw J wink at me.
                    He drives his usual
              slow pace, and a donkey-cart with paintings
on its panels of knights and palatins, driven by a woman
                    who looks like
              Orlando's mother careens in front, finocchi bound
like fasces bounce and sway, radishes the size of beets
                    roll about
              as she swerves to avoid potholes and pits.
W curses in German and honks. "Cigarette!"
                    he calls to J who
              pushes in the dashboard lighter. When it pops out
she hands it to him. It's at his lips before
                    he screams
              and drops it in his lap, slamming on the brakes.
"*Mistück!*" J turns round to look at me,
                    knowing my thoughts.
              A woman walks by in a large black straw hat,
from the top of which the white head of a cockerel
                    protrudes and,
looking about, crows.

RESTORATION OF A COPY OF AN IMAGINARY PAINTING

> *"......dire, non pas tout crûment sa vision, mais par un transfert instantané,*
> *constant, l'écho de sa présence."*
>
> — Victor Segelen

The white is meant to stabilize the house, but the matted crenelation
of reed-thatch throws it off to the side
until a squadron of crows solidifies the rhythm, carrying the eye through
incendiary doors to open space, opening it to the ancient, that is to say, the habitation
of sun and moon, the interior to the south, above the river that flows
by persimmon trees, over a statue with arms encircling a trunk, so you're not sure
who's upholding who, and the figure of someone silhouetted on a wall.
The month is September. Roses turn to the right,
and fail. Silent women in white blouses file by. But just at that moment when
the main matter seems to be about to be represented as rain and wings in a dark garden
and a bull bellowing, words like those that descended on the apostles are heard.
The copyist may have been about to make each tongue say the same thing,
but now it is too late. Everything before restoration is an unproven fact.
Everything after is guesswork.

THE FOUNTAIN
Istanbul 1970

In memoriam Yaşar Kemal, 1922?-2015

"My mother was Circassian, born a slave, ashamed of my darkness.
'That's what happens when you marry a Turk'," she said. The door opens.

A man in a leather apron enters carrying a basket. "Today you are lucky.
Cherries have come, and peaches." The window opens to the south wind

backing up sludge. Beyond is the misty skyline of the Golden Horn.
She goes into the kitchen, comes back with a pie, "sour cherry."

"I will call Kemal for you." She dials, speaks, waits, puts the phone down.
"The exchange says he's changed his number. We all do. Have to."

She cuts the pie with a dagger. "He was sent to me. Lots of people are,
like you. He arrived at seven a.m., peasant time, 1951. His Kurdish

goat-felt jacket stank. That's the same stiff coat Paul begged Timothy
to bring him in jail. He stayed over a week. No concept of a visit."

An electric muezzin goes off. She pushes herself up from the chair.
"I'll try again." Same result. It's time to go. "Don't mention me by name,

and don't write about this visit. Next time I may not be so lucky.
If you want to meet again, it should be in Üsküdar, out in the open,

across from the ferry in Kabataş, by the fountain. I will try to bring him."
"Is it safe?" "He doesn't care. For a writer, he says, looking over your
shoulder is suicide. I will call you. Say *nevede çeşme?* Where's the fountain?"

For Mina Urgan

THE VISIT

Communists are "*Commune-ists*", Ankara still "*Angora.*"
Her dearest wish is a Paddington apartment. As she talks
I look out from the rose-draped balcony under volutes, corbels,
lattices, through a huge pylon to tankers battling currents,
hammers and sickles on smokestacks. Trusting their own pilots,
they make a habit of ramming old wooden mansions, *yalis.*
Beside them wooden fishing boats bob like new moon arks.
" I put our own lemon juice in the jam to make it set. You can
still get strawberries from Arnavutköy." A newspaper lies open
at a street protest. "If students want guns I'd send them to the army.
They'd have guns then. When I first arrived Turkey was more romantic,
all fezzes and veils. Now I expect they'll soon burn down the *yali*
next door. The owner won't sell. They've burnt down all the others
and put up concrete terraced buildings. Excuse me." She waddles
to the phone, dials, slams it down, curses in Cockney Turkish.
"I've tried calling the grocer all day for strawberries. I'm ready
to throw the phone out the window. They brought a Froggie
in to mend the system. 'Ah, beautiful! Beautiful!' he said. 'Perfect.
Just leave it alone.' So now you can't use the damn things.
They're all dead. Everything's dead. Did Yildez tell you her
theater earnings have dropped to half under martial law? She's
too thin, married too young, works too hard. My other children–
my husband was a pasha–I met him when I was an actress.
His father was pro-British and sent him over to study electrical
engineering and marry an English girl. When Turkey went with
the Axis powers he had a heart attack and died. I was just a girl
when I arrived. They used to catch so many fish just over there
they had to throw them back. Do you like green fig conserve?
They still chuck back tomatoes. They don't know how to can them...
Ah, Turan!" She introduces me. He points to a stain on his
new white suit trousers. "Always look before sitting," he says,
sitting wearily. After a while he says, "Finally they're going
to produce my dramas on classical themes. Part one is 'Ibrahim
the Lunatic.' I'd been banned for criticizing Atatürk. But now
I've disguised him in my seventeenth-century trilogy, 'The Theme
of Power.' If they see through it I'm done. I must make a phone call."

As he rises into the light, scars shine on face and hands. I hear
him dial, curse, slam the phone down. He returns with a bottle
of Fruka. "Wrong number. A canteen and an earful of abusement.
You can't trust the phone." They start to talk in Turkish. I look over
the balcony. Seagulls. Cumuli accumulating. And below everybody
doing something. I settle on a woman staggering under a bag of
bloody bones, and a man crossing the street strapped to a huge
pane of glass, looking as if at every step he is about to fall, but
righting himself, stumbling, rights himself, staggers.

HISTORY

"Sangre y palabras
Dejamos a nuestra hijos"
– Homero Aridjis

The craftsmen picked a feather carefully and placed it,
   from green birds, yellow birds, from jade brought out the jade,
from gold the gold, bejeweled the sun, wove the glow of brittle jade,
   from the flower brought out the flower, turned flayed skin to flowers
where now mothers sit in rebozos, babies at the breast, among
   child beggars, parrot-colored taxis, black armored vans, pink crosses
on black telephone poles until the wailing around midnight, the moon out
   in back streets where a veiled woman in white walks beside girls
who'd wept as priests cut their throats and laid their bodies in
   the lake's whirlpool that swirled the blood away with jewels, stones,
gold, before people in silence returned to the city with its rubble
   from the wake still in the streets where a young girl in a shawl sits
on the sidewalk selling lizards beside me on a bench reading *Poesia*
   Indigena where beings and things diffuse, beauty and blood fuse,
while over my head ripening fruits are light taken in and shaped to fit
   their own shadows falling over me with at my feet tranced flowers
yellow, red and white, mottled like the thighs of the divine mother
   who was painted with chalk and fed deer hearts, for whom men danced
in feathers then turned to deer that went to live on the high barren plain
   whose music is echoic so I can hear it over the hubbub, over the cathedral
that is a temple ransacked and remade, and I think of how we invent
   our selves and spread them out, before, behind, flayed thin, skins we
live in to dream. When I look up, there's a great bird, engulfed in sky,
   leaving marks to be read like back-fires or the after-images of flame.

ORIGIN MYTH

— *Florentine Codex*, bk. 10, ch. 29

Good maguey they found that made good aguamiel.
His mother found it, Mayahuel. She also found firewater.
Johnny Walker, it was called, Dimple, Pinch, Cutty Sark.
Cuextecatl the *tlatoani* drank it. He wouldn't share.
He asked for more, and more, until he stood up, tore off
his breechcloth, too out his "divinity" and waved it about
like a prayerstick so the elders expelled him and Mayahuel
and his whole family, so he drank a lot and never again
wore breech clouts, even in bed, just pajama tops, no bottoms
so his divinity swung before him for all to see and they all
had to worship his divinity, and his wife became addicted
to enemas and netti pots and his daughter cut herself but
his son was afraid and for a present made up a box of songs
for his father. "Wake," said one, "the flames have risen.
Dawn is here. The flame-colored pheasant is calling, the flame-
colored swallow is flying and the flame butterfly is passing by."
But his father tore it open, then threw it across the floor.
"I thought it was a box of Montecristos," he said. And the son
in piety blew onto paper and burned it. But when his father
started to stick hairpins and knife-blades into his ears
and squeeze his nose red and pull out his eyelashes, when
his eyes turned puffy, teeth gray, wattles like a turkey,
the son made a polished mirror and held it to Cuextecatl's face.
But he knocked it aside and made his own mask of turquoise
snake teeth and quetzal feathers, and caught the train for the city,
promising never to return, but he did, again and again.

GHOSTS

Crossing the canal that led to the brackish lagoon, rain
stippling the surface a few marigold petals shivered on, a boat
came from the other side luminous as a monarch butterfly

while the festival behind lit fire after fire so the whole place
burned like an unhealed wound and as we passed we said nothing
for he was out of the pages of a book forever being written and I

his son, his washed-out palimpsest, a specter too, both making
the crossing as silhouettes, older than the surrounding mountains,
calm as if we didn't know each other and as I turned around

to watch his back, the tracks in the water were frayed cords
of the phone on which he called me to tell me to go to hell which
is where I went and where I found him again.

FIRE CEREMONY

One man, yellow and red, tasseled hat, green skirt ringed with seashells,
flayed skin draped over him, the face way down his back, genitals round
his neck, leading the other, chalk-white, tipsy, shorn head under plumed

headdress, hand in hand, "father" and "son," captor and captive, both
the same age, and one will tear out the other's heart and start a fire in
his chest and it will be beautiful, the world renewed, fresh fire in the blood,

carried everywhere to destroy the old, and the son will live in the Sun's retinue
as he flies down the steps to be gathered by the father, boiled and eaten with
squash flowers, finger-bones ringing like gourd rattles, head-nerve singing,

thighs planted firmly in the pot, a flower-tree, the flower, *ciucatl,* the song,
xochitl, flowers everywhere, delicious flowers, palms, hip bones, ribs, forearms,
soles of the feet, select parts for the gods and select friends, torches to light

the world and the sun itself, fathers and sons illuminated from within where
everything is at stake, father and sun united the way God before the beginning
of things used Himself as light, even before He said "Let there be light."

THE FLOWER WORLD

In the sedges and reeds of Chalco is the house of the gods, where day
and night a thrush trills, shining, while the petaled water stretches out
among the flowers, and there the quetzal bird sings too as the intoxicating
flowers bend to the sound of tambourines in praise of the Sun, who is here
in an urn with a turquoise collar, while rain blooms among the shadows
and the transvestites dance in bird costumes among flowers which are
the hearts and flesh of the gods we feed, for everyone is in the hands of
the Ruler of Death, who opens corollas and dries them up even here on
this vacant lot where everything's ablaze and the fire of destruction digs
deeper, eating through itself to the rust under everything, here where the
sanguinary scents of flowers turn to the stifling smell of concrete in the heat,
where cars feed roads and move like mirrors in and out of each other in front
of the Dominican church slaves built, where roofs with flickering aerials
turn aside in a sky further off than usual, thin clouds forming and reforming
as I lean against the blackened silk-cotton tree in the Place of Rains, near the
bus station on August 13, my birthday, the day Cortés captured Cuautemoc
in his torn finery, beside the market where headless things hang and flies hum
loud as the hummingbirds that move from one bright corpse to the other,
mistaking them for flowers and where fruits are carefully piled in pyramids on
which sit, here and there, butterflies opening and closing their wings like sails
and I recall on my way to school each gray morning stopping to gaze at the
incongruous glass door stained like a church window, from which a Spanish galleon
rose with billowing scarlet sails on cobalt waves out into the back lanes, over wet
cobbles toward the Tyne, past the Swan Hunter ship-yard, out to the North Sea.

NEW POEMS

212

THESEUS' SHIP

Garden abuzz with corn, beans, hives, ruby-throats,
everything behind or in front of an image of itself,

you can't tell one from the other, and all being
stolen, tree from tree, hill from hill, stream from stream,

from under our very noses where smell's now faint
as sight we'd counted on to make what is. Still,

I feel there are trees in front of me that taught us
how to think like trees, leafing, blossoming, dancing

ideas whose time has come but can't arrive and that's
what keeps them going, just as every time I look

into a cloudless sky, blue and more blue, and think
how beautiful, I am looking into emptiness and

the fullness of the self which, like Theseus' ship,
whose name we are never told, is always and never itself.

A WORD

Stumbling through tangled trees I tripped,
fell, came face to face with gold

disappearing through dust storms
of bees stuffing stony earth

with sweetness, pushing down past
each other, back up to fly through

an ultra-violet world where I was
boulder, stump, nothing, and I got

to my feet, pushed through ferns,
headed down, passing a pond where

a mallard was making final dives,
and I stopped to watch his almost

excessive beauty, admire each shake
of his shot-silk head scattering

galaxies, until light crumbled over
what seemed a man on the far bank,

transparent, mouthing over and over
a single word I could not make out.

WILD APPLES

Trees gnarled as that bronze Hellenic boxer, naked,
nose broken, teeth missing, tired, planted long ago
by the farmer and his wife and left when they could
no longer make a go of this thin soil and wild weather,
trees that crossed with others, or are throwbacks
to an ancestral stock tough as Neanderthals, whose
bruised and battered fruit with honey's aftertaste and
edge of citrus fall for deer, go off in their stomachs
so they stagger and dream, taint the air, drawing in
bears who mouth them whole, grubs and rot, and dance
with the spirits of the tree, heads alembics, looking up
at geese upside down singing their songs backwards or way
ahead, calling out to them "I miss you, miss you, wait!"

PLAIN AND SIMPLE

English is without gender, but our world still copulates
and words go at it with a will. Sometimes they do it
when you least expect, like sitting on a subway train,
or standing on a street. Words even manage to get it on
without a copula or conjunction in sight, falling over
a comma in their haste to consummate, throwing off
grammar like underwear, aiming at the naked truth.
Often they couldn't care less if their love-object is
boy or girl, neither or both. English once had gender,
but no more. So, so much for gender. Tenses are
another matter since time's a sorry thing and
whatever words may say you're still not sure if
something happened, is about to happen, or is happening,
let alone if past and future are where we say they are—
in some cultures the past is front and the future
behind. There is no tense for the sides and arounds
from which birdsong comes at you at the same time
in spring. And let us not forget nouns that for poets
could be verbs, "doing words," and verbs themselves
that move everything around, and adjectives that touch
and go, flit around like hummingbirds, even pronouns
that tighten things up but have little personality, and
the yets, howevers, neverthelesses and so on who keep
the game going in various directions like the wind that
skips over, around and across the pond I love, and where
I'm now sitting turning it to words flowing in, reflecting,
flowing out, the same and not the same with trout shivering
the surface and dragonflies dipping in, sending out
circles that break against banks and come back, and
I wish my dad was here so I could try again to answer
his question: "Why can't you just say what you mean,
say things the way they are, plain and simple?"

SIGHT LINE

I'd take you up the road and show you Picasso's "Tomato Plant"
  on my wall, but I won't. You don't really know me and you might not
recognize me since I've let my hair grow long in front and back as if
  I didn't know which way I was heading. But is the fool's walk
the only one that leads to enlightenment? And if so, as I sit on this rock
  why does day's last light leap around like an ibex? Is it signaling something
to me of great importance, or searching for something? Is it celebrating about
  to be extinguished and lost, as if getting lost would be achievement
when just about everyone and everything is lost, weighing on me with
  their absence so merely trying to think about them makes it worse?
And what of all those just waiting for words to make them whole again,
  as if I can remember anything I don't even know for sure existed?
I search for meaning which it's clear is hiding something, and so,
  it seems, am I. The person you see isn't the one here, or there.
Thinking all this might make me aware but not what I'm aware of.
  Life is not a diary or journal. It's flowing and flashing all over the place,
which is how I just recalled leaning my head over the top of the stairs
  years ago and calling into the empty well for my mother. "Oh," I said,
"I'm sorry. I'll go away. I'll get a grip. I'll try harder. I'll try someone else."
  Which I did, and that's how I came across art's waking dream with Picasso's
painting of a slightly droopy tomato plant in a funny-shaped pot,
  leaning against window-panes, three small fruit, one ripe, two not,
stem tied with twine to a stick, this sun-dappled painting going nowhere
  that spoke to me. So, yes, I'd like to share it, if it's still there, but
I think I'll sit here a bit longer on this large boulder, a granite erratic
  among flat bluestone, brought vast distance from who knows where
in an ice-sheet and dropped here all by itself when the energy left
  the ice. I'm looking about for markers to show me more than myself,
searching from a fixed point in a sea of green and sky since the longer
  the sight-line the more accurate the observation here at the head of
this valley near the beaver pond where the beavers were shot out for
  making themselves too much at home, flooding the road and
cutting me completely off. I was the one who shot them but the road
  is still washed out. And I was the one who would have picked the last,
the only, red tomato, the one full of sun, broken the windows
  to let in more or for the plant to escape and play on its own terms
because here where I now sit light has died and the moon's just risen.

It is hard to make out her complicated movements which, so I read,
in one month echo the sun's year. It takes ten years to see her rise in all
   possible directions in her nineteen year cycle which produced great cultures
and stone circles and monuments that tried to contain time in the timeless.
   If this takes too long, and Picasso's not to your taste, I also have Constable's
"Salisbury Cathedral from the Meadows" above my desk though I seldom
   show it because it's very personal, intimate even, so much so it seems
to be projected inside my skull, flickering there, the church's great spire
   pointing clear, the rainbow stretching up and across storm clouds and
ending before the down-turn, out of sight. I pick out the little dog not even
   itself but quoted from another painting, and the bow-wagon dead center trailing
white impasto trails as if going somewhere and wanting to be tracked
   so it would know where it's been if not where it's going.

GRAY GARDENS

It just came at you. You were in it almost
    before knowing—but let me dispense with confessions
and tell the truth: It wasn't that great, the garden.
    It just appeared from the street, loomed up after
you'd reached the edges and limits of more of the same.
    You could even have been lost—"Tossed, why tossed?"
Lost. Once inside it seemed smaller—"Or larger." There were
    corners and benches handed over to nannies where
they talked on cell phones. No parents, just nannies who
    passed around their charges, some ending up in branches,
others safe in prams—"Baby carriages." Can't you shut up!
    Sometimes it snowed, sometimes it stormed, but nobody
seemed to think there was anything to worry about.
    "What about the child molesters?" Trees made it feel safe,
you were always in the shade and shadow of buildings
    through which wind made sounds like crying. Sometimes
sunlight made it through and groped around. It looked
    like hard work. "Work?" Yes, what you do to make
ends meet. "Why on earth would you want ends to meet?
    You'd go in circles." Forget it. "Can I ask you something?
No. "Why did you never marry?" Light slid around on the pond—
    "You never mentioned a pond"—like water-striders—
"Which are?"—shiny, fast, unpredictable beads and blobs
    who dash about on the surface as if they're after something.
"Can't you see why a pond in a place with children might
    not be such a good idea?" I can now. "A still mind is a calm,
deep pond." The mind's a grave. "With ghosts." Why
    do people have kids if they hand them over to strangers
almost as soon as they're born? Families are no more,
    "What do those beetles actually *do*?" Who knows. I said
they were light on the pond. Metaphor. Flashing all over
    like scattered thoughts of a broken mind. "Simile.
Have you ever been in love?" They look like they live
    in constant anxiety, they can't keep still. "Can they fly?"
I don't think so. "Then they're trapped." They look like
    shooting stars, or quick constellations. Some sink.
"Some shall not be saved. St. Paul." They're like pieces

on a Ouija board—"There are no pieces on a Ouija board—"
spirits summoned to give direction, help me cross a street
    without looking both ways every which way, again and again,
unable to move—"Have you never loved anyone?"—and go
    to my own house, my home with its own entrance.
"En*trance?*" OK, en*trance*, a place of wonder, wife, children,
    a kind of fulfilment, where each thing means itself, no confusion,
echoes—"Geckos, you say?" OK. By now, one word's as good
    as another. Tire-marks will do as well as truth. "You had your chance."
We have nothing more to say. The garden closes—"gardens close"—
    early and empties—"empty—fast. It's lonely and scary in the dark.
"In light too." Be quiet. "Silence assails all, in the end."

JOURNAL, OR STORY WITHOUT WORDS

And I follow the hand copying what it had written years ago,
never knowing it would survive and mean something other,

perhaps even more, than it had intended, from history as
record to history re-conceived, re-purposed, not as knowledge

but a divining of underpinnings, the person-in-process becoming
never-was or to be what-became-of-him looking back

from the place where he'd looked toward but which was
no longer there or still uncreated and in the creation absorbing

what had gone before and turning in on itself, the writing
coming unstuck, its nails loosening, pulling with it part

of the wall, syntax spilling all over the place, a ghost dance
hoping to scrub the present clear, bring back the never there,

desired all the more for that. And now all this is lying in wait,
in ambush at the tips of my fingers, in the fingers themselves,

from a child's join-up letters to cursive to the scrawl and callus
time makes, hastening, abbreviating, cutting corners

till what you see is a virtual unintelligible you that grew out of itself,
though something unveils you, writes you the way God thought

the world in letters of the word which, we found out, can mean
just about anything and we had to supply our own thought,

the way the riddler Daniel supplied his own Aramaic vowels
to make what he needed for the writing on the wall, or the way

I found decades-old pages I thought were in my father's hand
but were in mine, I'd absorbed him, he was the source, wrong

as it turned out, the way Pliny held the waters of the Mediterranean
derived not from the Straits of Gibraltar but from the Black Sea

since the tide always flowing out of there never ebbs, pages
I later found when they was barely legible having been dropped

overboard on the Galata ferry, run over by Taurian bandits,
ransomed from a Trastevere urchin who found it in the river's mud

after everything I had was stolen and, nothing worth, dumped,
then again lost and found in the malarial swamp that had once been

the inland lake and harbor of Rhegura, and which I saved to be able
to write this up from words I can not or barely make out,

some in languages I didn't or no longer know, which can
mean a number of things, or nothing, in a story without words.

THE FENS, 1630s

Heavy damp blue smoke loses its way among bending reed and rill, from
heaps of turved hassocks, where they've readied land for ridging to curb flood
and purify the air, he says, though come fall of leaf it will be fen again. For now,

bitterns boom, cow calls to calf, midges whine, mist catches on low bushes,
a thinning caul that covers causeways till the sun's fist scatters it where mere's
mist clashes against the sky Ely's towers probe, glare-white. Facing the mere,

on bare patches godwits caught in crown nets sit, silent, for market, catch a last
glimpse of rippling waves, a moorhen gliding in until her feet dig out a wake
pointing to cattle that hurry for a final watering before the drovers set them on

a southward track. A blue heron's fixed by his unblinking eye on the spot where
a fish leapt. If a wind could get on track it would still lack motive to move anything,
even the feather that just fell, or the stalled swallow-tail. This all means waters

muzzled by the projector, not to run like froward beasts. So the Dutchman says.
Free rivers governed, water kept within banks, then, on bail, let go by careful sluices,
caught and bridled, made to run in traces, common fens trapped, tamed by engines,

all to be land rich as before the Flood, foison for all, says he. But from the east,
a flash from the bank we'd burst, sluice and clow freed, bursts of blue where
flocks of teal skid in, dip necks, splash like fish, so water steals from light the way

winter turns water with sheer winds slicing straight from Muscovy that overnight
bring dead hand and killing fogs, time of hoar-frost fruits, water turned to
bone, world the essence it has ever been, cast still in the heart's core.

AN UNFINISHED NUDE

On the turntable is Mahler's "Song of the Earth,"
Dunkel ist das Leben ist der Tod.
He lies back on the unmade camp-bed, inhales
a Nazionale, sips Fernet from a filthy glass,
belches, "dunkel indeed," recites Li Po:
A wine party./ I lay in a drowse./ Blown flowers fell
and filled my lap./ When I woke, still drunk,/
the birds all gone to their nests,/ I was drifting along
the river alone in the moonlight. The needle sticks.
He stretches out in the black, threadbare suit
he never sheds, head on a bag of clothes
the Swedish girl left three months back when he
gave her my money to pay the rent and she never returned.
He closes his eyes, a hollow laugh. "I can't get angry,
my lord," says this Donatello, this Faun of Praxiteles,
satyr recumbent, Nam recusant, *apolide* king here
in his ghetto "House of Lords," who seldom eats and
never washes, who hands out titles like cigarettes.
Bottles, fiaschi, cigarette cartons, garter belts, poems,
empty paint tubes all over the floor. He hasn't had
much sleep the last week on the roof avoiding Lady Loretta,
the Trotskyite mother of his son who will turn out
not to be his. Beside a poster she left--"Bruciamo
il Vaticano con il papa dentro./ Benzina, benzina
alle chiese"—propped against the window overlooking
the ghetto is an unfinished nude on a canvas, much
overpainted, draped with a ragged t-shirt.

                    In memoriam, Edward Bendel

COZUMEL

And there you are, Frida, mi amor, in your "Self-portrait
with cropped hair" which I have framed and mounted on the wall,
where you've decided to cut it all off, precious thick black braids,
so now it covers everything, everywhere, bits of yourself twisting,
drifting, drooping all over, over you too seated in a chair
in his suit and shirt, no more Tehuana skirts, scissors open
on your lap beside a dangling tuft. The suit's too big, hair
too short for your marmot face. You've cut yourself off,
for love, for love? Even your winged eyebrows don't look right,
nor your faint moustache, your too obvious earrings and
small feet too small for your small high-heel shoes.
But yes, you're still perfect, magical, I don't know what
you mean and don't care, you're you: *Mira que si te quise,*
fué por el pelo. Ahora que estás pelona, ya no te quiero.
But te quiero, Frida, I mouth back, here where I look at you
each day, I know you know, and I know you know I want
your excess, your artifice of passion, and to that end
I carry and lay before you this small basket of beeswax and
bitter honey, the same the natives brought Cortéz at Cozumel.

THE RETURN OF COYOTE
Coyote Sighted in Central Park
                    –"New York Times" headline.

Yea, that's me, spiky hair blowin' in the wind, tight black
    fish-net stockings almost cutting me in half, looking in through
their open penthouse window to a world like an installation
    made of hedge funds, real-estate mergers and junk bonds,
me drooling at the laden board in front of a big Basquiat
    with horns and Giacometti's "L'Homme au Doigt," while
Tony Bennett and Lady Gaga drift out and over Central Park.
    Sure, I'd like to blow it all up, but it would all come crashing down
on my head, like when I scattered the stars, and I can't suppress
    a bar or two of "Oh, Happy Day" because it's as if God
lived up here, though if He were a celebrity He'd be better known,
    I think, until I'm distracted by a whiff of "Joy"and the sparkle
of Chateau d'Yqem, but this time can't suppress a howl of
    delight so I have to slip off and drop down onto Park Avenue,
a shadow of flaps and patches, pulling my fedora over my pink
    pussy hat, head-phones piping in Jay Z or Monteverdi,
trotting on down to Wall Street where I give them my version
    of Giacometti's finger, squeeze the Charging Bull's balls,
pinch the Fearless Girl, sell a tourist a bottle of 9/11 air, hang out
    with Crusties and their pit bulls until a cab flattens me, wipe-out,
but I pop back up, a bit wobbly, climb back on, after all, I made
    life then death so you'd take life seriously even though
what I plan seldom turns out. I play my parts, double as myself,
    multi-me, my own marplot. Anyways, off I go again, sniffing things out,
a scat here, a piss there, just truckin', hungry as hell though I make
    even concrete yield something, here where the traffic's terrible
and crowds worse. Return? I never left, and if we survive all this,
    or even if we don't, I'll still be looking for you, and so, bella,
ciaou! Allons! I toss my red bandiera over my shoulder and set off.
    Though I have no idea where I'm going I'll get there. And if
you haven't already forgotten me, and still want to find me, look
    under your boot-soles, and take it from there. But what do I know,
que sais-je? If you believe this you'll believe anything, so let's leave
    this story where it is and start another

ELEGIAC

WINDOWS ASKEW

*

Peepers, greens, bullfrogs fading as a thrush sings on a rung
beside the wind-chimes. A robin sits on the empty feeder

looking around. The maples' red twigs hang above the over-
grown garden, and again I watch her drift along stone walls,

under the huge, battered line-trees whose cracked limbs still
sprout red florets delicate as orchids. But she is not looking at them,

and not back at me, as she turns off near the abandoned
farmhouse held up by planks and briers, its lone carp rising

gold through water that was ice, coming up slow, like a question
to which there is no answer, and she's gone.

*

In the dry stream-bed a porcupine, scratching, working himself over,
moaning. Soon I'm scratching too, both of us moving with

the dull monotony of grief. He makes no concession to silence,
shaking his quills, sniffing bark until, half-hearted, balanced on his

earthbound tail, he starts heaving himself up a tree, but falls
back in a heap, spinning round to see who did this to him, then

comes straight at me, sniffing the air, tiny eyes not much help,
groaning as if everything hurt, and I groan too as he trundles

past like I wasn't there, before shooting up unstable scree,
still scratching, grief transformed to speed, and he's gone.

*

Anonymous still, I make do with feints and figments, fragments
in light eerie as phosphorescence from the split-fish or pilot-whale

strips we'd watched them hang, looked through to the Dipper's
seven stars and its bear tracks heading past the pole-star sitting

like a quail's egg. Sadness everywhere like air under a butterfly,
barely keeping it afloat.

*

Fresh drifts, shifting integrities, snow losing itself
in the shape it inherits, here where our house endures,

wood warped, windows askew in a trance of sunlight
acute as absence. A sort of duress keeps everything

in place, a structure from which has passed the desire
to be something else so there's nothing for shadows

to feed on, make more, or less, here where light lives
trapped in mirrors and her glass figurines so they're

still on fire, here where nebulae spill over old boards
and furniture memory grows from like old flowers, and

the pole star turns above logs in the hearth, maple and cedar,
cherry smooth as eelskin, everything its own emptiness, here.

A BIRD

The streambed's strewn with garbage and broken bottles.
A torn shirt hangs from an uprooted tree and—a flash,

you can't tell what as morning grinds out light,
and I remember a hummingbird in the grass here,

holding it up to my breath that ruffled its feathers
so they shone the way thought can glimmer and

be gone. I push open the garden gate one last time,
pick a small jade tomato, let drop. A chickadee hangs

upside down in the bare shadblow that snowed
each spring. I listen: a bird-song, silver wave on wave,

dying away like breath from a mask. I try repeating it
in case it wasn't there.

SPECTRUM

Dawn veers over the mountain, down
steep pastures broken by stone walls, through

stunted juniper and low thornbush into the house
where cluster-flies wake in sunlight and scream

at high windows to be let out. Days still demand,
so I get up, make the bed, drag the comforter

over where she used to lie though now each
morning when I reach over nothing's there. But

I feel she will return, lie down, get up, rhyme
with table, chairs, floor, the spectrum split

on the ceiling, over walls, from the crystal candlesticks
she won and which, in the dark, still work.

THE PHOTO

The watch goes off in my desk. I open my eyes
to the photo of her standing on the stoop,

each morning looking back at me. Out the window,
nothing moves until a bird flits by, no sound until

a dove mumbles and a gun fires, just as the compressor
in the fridge goes crash. I see a spider moving across

the ceiling, a wolf-spider, the kind that jump from ambush.
Another is hiding behind the photo. All night coyotes

howled beneath the window until I dreamed them,
wild and hungry roaming through town. The photo moves.

I see her on the stoop that still needs fixing. The steps
are loose. They'll stay that way.

THE WAIT

The time has come, says my wife, startling me,
    but all she means is that she's going to clean out
        the linen closet. She says it calms her down.

I have been waiting for the call to tell me whether
    I live or die, more or less. So far, I'm alive,
        distracting myself with anything, settling on

organizing bookshelves where *The Cloud of Unknowing*
    sits next to *Gray's Anatomy*, *The Encyclopedia*
        of Ignorance next to the Bible, and I watch

the clock that doesn't move, try to focus, look for
    alliances so as not to get lost, can't stop, as if any pause
        means end, you cannot push back that hole

in front of you, coming at you as you ride the wave
    of heartbeats to count as if they will be gone soon
        when the horizon slips off the end as it did

for ancient sailors in their weak vessels on the unknown,
    up, down, hot, cold, waiting for it to *ring, ring,*
        ring, why doesn't he call? Thank god he doesn't

call. I count the poppies on the cushion to hang my
    mind on something, red, red, flowing fields of
        poppies. I rearrange desk and shelves as if

they were my life, reach down again, get hung up
    again on *The Human Body*, page 148, "coronary
        arteries", and think how useless it all is, knowledge,

and when the call finally comes it is the ghostly hand
    beckoning into the unknown which is where
        I've been and where I'll go again.

THE DIAGNOSIS

A cave, deep inside, animals painted with
   their own blood, until I woke and sat again
      across from the sofa, lights at foot

and head over waves of blue cushions with
   poppies, damask roses, heart's ease, grapevines,
      a veritable paradise, a lost world, and along

the sofa back small Indian cushions with tendrils
   and arabesques, inlaid mirrors that watch as I watch
      where she will sit, reading, legs drawn up, while

I try to rest my mind in the nest she makes, pretend
   to read, in fact watching as she reads, looking over
      at me when she thinks I am not looking, checking

if I am still carrying myself like a thin glass bowl while
   outside frost like anguish pushes up great clods,
      stones, sticks, roots embedded, gripped so tight

it hurts, can't breathe and among those blue billows
   I see again the Blue Whale who lost control
      of his own body, entered the killing zone and beached,

died there vena cava to crawl through, aorta you could
   lodge in, heart "the size of a deflated swimming pool,"
      which they "excavated" and hauled off in a front-loader,

"freeing" it, replace its fluids with silicone polymers,
   "plastinates" for the museum, there forever as something
      else in a blank ocean.

CARDIAC

Echoes bounced about in what
   was me, drifted through lava tubes,

   along streams and well-trodden
paths cluttered with debris of storms

and careless campers. Am I asleep?
   I dress and stretch as if I haven't lived,

   stand and watch myself walking along
a path where a purple flower pulses.

The boy I left sleeping, abandoned to the
   tall grass, wakes too, rises, picks up his bike,

   climbs on, pumps hard, falls off, gets on, pushes
through moonlit shadows, listens to hear,

thinks he can, careful not to fall off,
   again.

SPRING CLEAN

I've emptied drawers, files and shelves. A clean
break I say as I pack in the first batch, letters
from the living, epistles from the dead, tax returns,
journals, certificates, clippings, drafts, manuscripts,
cremate the lot, I think, the house too if I could, but
I've jammed them in so tight no air can get among them,
nothing will take, each corner I light flares, splutters,
dies. So I grab the poker, fluff it all up best I can,
and it takes, eats a poem, quits. I try again again,
poke, lift, turn, light, flare and fade. I quit. Now what?
Try again. A brief blaze, roar, but the pile seems
more not less. Sometimes bits of scorched paper
fly into the room before I can clamp the door fast.
The whole place stinks of smoke. Exhausted, I try again,
strike my last match, touch it to a page whose corner
catches, lifts, a thin red line blows back along itself
glowing in the dark, an ignis fatuus that curls up soon
and dies. I could unpack it all, burn it slowly page
by page, but I might be tempted to read, and what
would be the point of that? So I give up, close up,
call it quits. In the morning, half-awake, to see if anything
has happened while I slept, I slowly open the stove.
A blast of air rushes down the chimney, hurling a
simoom of paper, dust and ashes into my face. I can't
breathe, can hardly see but it's all still there, squat
and dense as the past, its own pace. I try to shut the door.

THE ETERNAL RETURN

In fall I stomp, bomb and spray them with worse than
agent-orange. They fall as black rain on soup and sinner

alike. And still they come. The locals say, *Just sweep 'em up.*
I do, again and again, and by first snow they're gone.

In spring I find cluster-fly nurseries in riddled cowpats and think,
well, maybe this year they've gone somewhere else, and

I forget them. Until fall when they seep in again through
cracks and they're everywhere, crawling up windows to

the sun, clustering as satanic clots in corners. Then they fall,
hit the floor singing high-pitched death-songs, dog-soldiers

staked to the spot, spinning on their backs, break-dancing,
flailing legs of thread, flapping mica wings, coming apart.

So I sweep them up, toss them out into the cold where
they will sleep their sleep, dream the same dream all winter

till in spring it comes true again, and they wake, born of dung
to no end save that which made them, serious as the sun into which

they vanish, to return, reconstituted, unresolved.

POETRY AND BIRDS

At Cambridge in the early '60s, my poetry curriculum began in about the eighth and ended, for the most part, in the early nineteenth century. But when I was about seventeen, in high school I'd happened upon William Empson's *Seven Types of Ambiguity*, along with the poetry of Thomas Hardy and Robert Graves. Empson, soon to be joined by I. A. Richards, quickly became a favorite with his revelation of the resonant possibilities of the poem itself (parenthetically, Stanley Burnshaw's *The Poem Itself* and *The Seamless Web* are two of my favorite books). As for Hardy, I absorbed everything I could find, poetry and fiction, while Graves' poetry and prose transported me into a mythic wonderland, especially when supplemented by *The Golden Bough* (in college, for six pence I picked up James Frazer's own inscribed copy of Lady Charlotte Guest's *The Mabinogion*, and still treasure it). Even today I can remember the excitement I felt reading my extra-curricular discoveries. People have described this sensation in different ways. Matthew Arnold, for example, described it as a "vibration," a shiver up the spine. I don't claim to feel quite the same youthful sensation today, no matter how much enjoyment I experience. However, thinking about this essay and searching about for ways to describe that early excitement, I recalled an incident from some years ago when I was staying on Ossabaw Island off the coast of Georgia. A friend had trained his high-powered binoculars on a large Spanish moss-bedizened live oak and waved me over. Pointing, he handed me his glasses. "There!" he whispered, and, after some excited searching—there indeed! I had never seen anything like it. My sight was flooded and filled with colors there's no point in trying to portray. The richness, the vision took me over. A well-named nonpareil or painted bunting! A tiny bird that now seemed as big as my brain. I did not want to hand the glasses back. The bird solved my dilemma by flying off. If I didn't want to sound overly dramatic, even clichéd, I'd say that for an instant it took my breath with it. I was transported.

* *

True poetry exists in the engendering dark, giving and receiving light. The language of poetry resonates like whale-song. The words shimmer with their long journeys, their history. They echo their past at their core and around the edges where they flicker with suggestiveness, elusive linkages, which is why translation is only successful when equivalent echoes are created. Words live from their roots. Cut off, they are just implements. It is good for poets to know some etymology, some linguistics, the history of the language, and of the words they work with whose roots are deep in our ancient being, perhaps pre-alphabetical and even pre-linguistic, from a time using "a mode of thought based on diffuse multidimensional configurations," (André Leroi-Gourhan), a way of consciousness using "things to think with" (Claude Lévi-Strauss). Words in poetry are living tissue. A word is, radically, breath, something spoken. It is muscular, physical. It is, to use R.P. Blackmur's term, "gesture."

* *

If true poetry lives in the dark, it also lives in space, in reverberative vacancy, so visual and auditory intelligence is called for. The page's wholeness is air, its life emptiness. Here words can rise from the linear plane and inhabit whiteness, floating but not free, for there is no such thing as free verse any more than there is free movement; movement is constrained and shaped by structure. A poem's "plot" is its trajectory. The precise knit, the corruscation of imagery, the flow and break of rhythm, the expectation and frustration, the music, polyphonic pulse and breath, these make up the poem's connective tissue, its "seamless web", its body, what it looks, feels and sounds like, its "*idea,*" (from the PIE root meaning "to look"), its "*meaning,*" (from OE "maenan", "to tell, recite, speak"); these two words point to the shape, the breathing-speaking. There is nothing to "prove," though there is everything to demonstrate. An idea in a poem is something "thoroughly incarnate," in George Eliot's phrase, its wisdom to be known and understood by looking deeply, the way of the "seer." "I see" and "I understand" are synonymous, but "understand" is a mysterious word, (contrast another synonym, the latinate and abstract "comprehend.") This deceptively simple word evokes almost a mythic memory, something like the central sacrificial Mithraic rite where an initiate *stood under* the grill and was drenched, bathed in the blood of the bull, transformed. The best way to understand the "meaning" of a poem is to stand under it, soak it in, be trans- and re-formed. Perhaps with this word we can see an example of what Ernst Cassirer in *Language and Myth* termed "the bond between linguistic and mytho-religious experience," expressed in the fact that verbal structures appear as "mythical entities" where the word becomes "a sort of primary force."

* *

In today's vernacular, the verb "to say" has become the verb "to go"–"I went [said], he went [said]." What Logan Pearsall Smith years ago in *The English Language* termed "the genius of the Language" has understood words as actions. Similarly, a word in a poem is an event (compare Hebrew "dabar", which means both "word" and "event"). The "life-world" of a poem is never remote, felt "reflexively." The expression of a truth is sensed as itself always as a happening, though you can't count on a poem to complete itself while you're there. The poem enacts its own being. It dances its own attitudes. It is Wallace Stevens' "gaiety of language," which is very different from Yvor Winters' definition of a poem in *The Function of Criticism* as "a rational statement" where emotion is "communicated simultaneously with rational understanding," creating "a judgment." Such a poem would be without ambiguities, fully paraphrasable, with no "irrational" elements. To me, however, the language of poetry is not transparent. You can't see through it to a prose "meaning," though prose can sometimes limp behind with a flashlight. There is just more body, more poem, (we talk of "the body" of a poem); there is more "spirit," to use Kant's word, more beauty "born of the spirit and born again," where *spirit* is the invisible vitalizing force of breath, *spiritus,* mind-breath, continuous, animating and re-animated by another's sensibility. In a way, adapting

240

Beloit Mandelbrot's concept of fractals, one might even talk of the "self-similarity" of poems, their "meaning" or "plastic beauty" being "a richness of possibility" (*The Fractal Geometry of Nature*). Or one might say that "meaning" in poetry occurs when ambiguities focus and balance dynamically so they strain their bonds and almost seem to be about to break free, like Michelangelo's prisoners. Or one could also note the importance of the lyric's musical component which, as Eugenio Montale said, can make a poem's "meaning" slippery, hard earned, as one tries to reconcile the "literal meaning" and "the musical sense," since the two can present different degrees of incompatibility (or compatibility), between "rational import," which may be "evident," and the verbal music which can be "secret, concealed, almost beyond our grasp" (afterword to Lucio Piccolo's 1956 volume *Canti barocchi*). In this vein, Christopher Middleton once wrote me that "a poem, or line, has to have a phonic shape which points toward some kind of psychic thing beyond 'thought'." This "phonic" "psychic thing" could be what John Ashbery was alluding to in a 1991 interview where he said that, "words in proximity to one another take on another meaning. What you hear at a given moment is a refraction of what's gone before or after." His "hear" points to the auditory/ musical, while "refraction" suggests an a-temporal reverberance, echoic and even integrally incomplete.

Poets have often stressed the importance of music and voice, the sound of a poem, and C.K. Williams even said that "meaning" arrives after the music has been established and, mysteriously, is contained in it ("On Whitman: The Music"). For me, music is of the essence. It is not some "amoral sonic pleasure," a "system of cultivated sounds" which Wayne Koestenbaum in a 2016 *New York Times Book Review* claimed Adrienne Rich repudiated as part of "a patriarchal racket." To my mind, "meaning" has to include commitment to sound and texture as well as the dimensions of thought and feeling, and even be open to chance since in a poem words can change meanings, acquire modulations as they reflect and react to each other, threads of accident in the lattice of "meaning." It all has to do with the weaving of the *text*, the polyphonic mesh, something sensuous, a fabric you can hold and wear, taste, smell, see (remember Denise Levertov's *O Taste and See*, 1964), and think about; a tangible intangibility that is, a being ("the poem is a sort of animal," said Ted Hughes) that expresses itself in kinds of congruity, since words are "things…active and efficient" (Wordsworth, Note to "The Thorn").

* *

It could be that the search for "meaning" is the reason so many intelligent people find poetry "difficult." Today, poetry may not be just the skilful re-expression of familiar or general truths or sentiments, "what oft was thought, but ne'er so well expressed." But it is still available to anyone ready to engage it on its own terms, prepared to be prodded and enticed out of familiarity with self and world, even with language and poetry itself. All that is required is a sense of and taste for emotional and intellectual adventure, an openness to risk, even in those scary cases where "the reader is placed in an unprecedented condition of estrangement from his reading habits" (Pasolini on Zanzotto). An ability to tolerate or even enjoy uncertainty and ambiguity is helpful, perhaps essential, since a poem is almost always about something else, as befits its close relationship with riddle, one of "the roots of lyric" (Andrew Welch), a connection which Susan Brind Morrow claims goes back at least four thousand years to the poetic riddles of the Egyptian "Pyramid Texts." Though Jan Huizinga in *Homo Ludens* doubts that contemporary civilization is capable of appreciating and nurturing poetry's "special language," he notes that this relationship with riddle "is never entirely lost," tracing it back to the Greeks who "required the poet's word to be dark," to the Icelandic *skalds* who considered "too much clarity" to be "a technical fault," and to the troubadours for whom "special merit was attributed to the *trobarclus*–the making of recondite poetry." Riddle, after all, as Aristotle pointed out, is metaphor, which means we can never really know what something *is* because we are defining it by what it isn't, knowing it by its connections, changing it, carrying it across, trans-lating, trans-porting it (Greek "metafora" signifies "carrying across"). So "meaning" is "process." Perhaps Emily Dickinson's riddling lines say it best: "And through a Riddle, at the last– / Sagacity, must go."

* *

Poetry is much older than prose. It does not create "isolated mental entities or abstractions" (Eric Havelock, *Preface to Plato*) to describe the world objectively and impersonally. It generates a physiology, a tangible thick world of imagistic continuity via sensual pleasure, making it difficult for us to separate ourselves from it, which was the reason Plato rejected it, insisting on abstract language to describe and explain experience, thus bringing us closer to pure "forms," invisible ideals which artists degrade and distort. In addition, following Havelock, Walter J. Ong has pointed out how in oral-aural cultures words are more "celebration," "events," "happenings" and less "tools," or "work." This is still true of that poetry today which keeps close contact with the core. And this core seems to exist in a deep part of the brain where "thinking" works apart from logic, not divorced but in a different register, where connections are made quickly, as perhaps they were at a time when quick and decisive action was a matter of life and death. It would be a mistake, however, to say there is no logic in poetry, no structure of reason, that it is all "emotion." For not only is there an intense logic of image, there is the particularization in the way components interact, projecting an "argument" that "adds up," that "makes sense." This includes the sorting and discriminating of hints and echoes, the evaluation of leads, calling for something like detective skills, the way of riddle. So yes, there is logic, but at heart poetry is an exploratory even tentative "knowing" embedded in its syntactical dance, open to "unknowing." It slips analytical philosophy's focus on that problematic part of our being we call "reason." Which does not make it unreasonable

* *

In oral cultures words are alive, part of a sentient world with human and other-than-human beings. They are "interactive," "participatory," as Dennis Tedlock and others have noted. Moreover, Native American oral narratives which used to be translated into prose as "stories" are now, following the lead of Tedlock and, in particular Dell Hymes, translated and presented as "poetry," into formats showing their complex rhythmic, dramatic and patterned structures. In this vein, it is interesting to note that narratives in oral cultures are often thought of as living entities. Among certain Algonquian-speaking people, for instance, the story is a person accustomed to walking all over the world whose story cannot be told until it stops and makes camp. It does what you do. It is what you are. There is no separation between what is told, who tells it, and you the listener. Curiously, this is something like the way I feel when I read a good poem: non-separation. I am drawn into it as into myself, as if it were part of me. I have the sensation that the poem is flesh, something palpable I can touch, grasp, and as I do so I become different (I experience a similar reaction in front of a beautiful painting, when I am somehow the movements, the shapes; they are inside me, a reciprocal physical fit).

* *

Plato somewhere describes the mysterious way in which, during the course of an ordinary day, we are attracted and moved by something we cannot explain or understand. The kind of poetry that means a great deal to me begins in and is rooted in the wonder of what Paul Falkowski calls our improbable, "almost magical" existence (*Life's Engines*), when, for example, something we might have seen a thousand times catches the attention and this time holds it. A tree, horses in a field, a sparrow on the sidewalk, a word, phrase or sentence, heard or read, or something we didn't know we had remembered bubbles up, or what the photographer Robert Frank characterized as "some moment I couldn't explain." Then the poem spins out reverberating images with the appearance and feel of permanence; it embodies a sensation, making a moment mysterious and valuable in our throw-away culture. Even when a poem is complete, however, it can never tell us everything it knows. It is always holding something back, the way of the dream. And poetry today re-enchants ("re-sings") the world in various ways, even when it reveals "the thingness of things," a world *in se,* as in Zbigniew Herbert's richly austere "The Pebble". But surrealism has been the most powerful response to the materialist 20th. Century. It has influenced all the arts with its central concept of "le merveilleux." "Only the marvelous is beautiful," wrote André Breton in 1924, and Louis Aragon added a couple of years later that it was "the eruption of contradiction within the real." In such ways poetry breaks and builds, mixes "as if" and "it is," *as if* becoming *it is* and vice versa. It re-phrases boundaries. It is "oceanic thinking" (Jean Gebser's phrase). It is "also" and "not only" whereas in "mental thinking" only "either-or" is valid. It is "as if" the world's vibratory field calls at unpredictable moments and in unexpected places. I remember Magritte who, after a visit to a working-class Brussels beer-hall, wrote that he found the door-moldings "endowed with a mysterious life," and he remained "a long time in contact with their reality." And when

William Carlos Williams saw a red wheelbarrow "outside the window of an old negro's house on a backstreet" in Rutherford he wrote that the sight impressed him somehow "as about the most important and most integral that it had ever been my pleasure to gaze upon." (Recently, I was glad to read that awe, wonder and beauty promote lower, healthier levels of cytokines, whose elevated levels are tied to depression). A poem lives in the numinous and, as Paul Ricoeur noted, becomes "the representation of a presence." The ancient world, like some traditional tribal cultures still today, was filled with presence, continually remaking itself. Poetry tries to call things back from the positivistic brink, away from what Rilke termed "America," where "empty, indifferent things pour over us." The history of the west is the removal of mind or spirit from phenomena. A poem calls us back to the world's beautiful strangeness, the uniqueness of everything and the way things are related, linked in a place at once us and not us.

* *

Philip Larkin once famously said, "Oh, for Christ's sake, one doesn't *study* poets! You read them, and think: 'That's marvelous, how is it done, could I do it?' And that's how you learn." Of course, that's true. But my experience of the marvelous in the form of a small bird led me to learn as much as I could about it, and that led me to an interest in ornithology. You can never know or learn too much, despite William Stafford's remark that you can be "too well prepared for poetry." I know what he means, but when you feel clogged up you can always go for a walk and keep an eye out for birds.

Brian Swann was born in Wallsend, England, in 1940, graduated as Foundation Scholar in 1963 from Queens' College, Cambridge, with a Double First in the English Tripos and came to Princeton in 1964 as a Proctor Fellow. After two years, he left for Europe, before returning in 1968 as a Princeton National Fellow, earning a PhD in 1970, and becoming a US citizen in 1980. He has published many books in a number of genres, from poetry and fiction to children's books, poetry in translation and Native American literature. He was founder and series editor of the Smithsonian Series of Studies in Native American Literatures and is founder and series editor of "Native Literatures of the Americas" for the University of Nebraska Press. He has won a number of awards and prizes, including a National Endowment for the Arts fellowship in fiction, the John Florio Prize for the best Italian translation published in the UK, and the Italo Calvino Award from Columbia University's Translation Center. In addition he won the University of Alabama Press open poetry prize for *The Middle of the Journey*, the Ohio State University Press *The Journal* prize for *Autumn Road*, the Miles Wever Todd Poetry Prize for *Snow House*, and the Autumn House Poetry Prize for *St. Francis and the Flies*. He has published six collections of short fiction, the most recent of which are *Dogs on the Roof* (MadHat Press, 2016) and *Not the Real Marilyn Monroe* (MadHat Press, 2017). His work has appeared in many scholarly journals, such as "English Literary History," "Novel," "Criticism," and "Nineteenth Century Fiction," as well as anthologies and literary magazines, including "New Republic," "The New Yorker," "Paris Review," "Hudson Review," "American Scholar," "Poetry," "Yale Review," "Harvard Review," "Raritan," "American Poetry Review," "Southern Review," and scores of others. His art work is represented by Pierogi Gallery in NYC. He has taught at Princeton and Rutgers and was director of the Bennington Writing Workshops. He is Professor of Humanities at the Cooper Union for the Advancement of Science and Art in New York City.

ALSO BY BRIAN SWANN

POETRY

The Whale's Scars, (New Rivers Press, 1975).
Roots, (New Rivers Press, 1976).
Living Time, (Quarterly Review of Literature Contemporary Poetry Series, 1978).
Paradigms of Fire, (Corycian Press, 1981).
The Middle of the Journey, (University of Alabama Press, 1982).
Song of the Sky: Versions of Native American Songs,
(University of Massachusetts Press, 1993).
Wearing the Morning Star: Versions of Native American Song-poems,
(Random House, 1996).
Autumn Road, (Ohio State University Press, 2005).
Snow House, (Pleiades Press/LSU Press, 2006).
In Late Light, (Johns Hopkins University Press, 2013).
St. Francis and the Flies, (Autumn House Press, 2016).
Companions, Analogies, (Sheep Meadow Press, 2016).

FICTION

The Runner, (Carpenter Press, 1979).
Unreal Estate, (Toothpaste Press/ Coffee House Press, 1981).
Elizabeth, (Penmaen Press, 1981).
Another Story, (Adler Publishing Co., 1984).
The Plot of the Mice, (Capra Press, 1986).
Dogs on the Roof, (MadHat Press, 2016).
Not the Real Marilyn Monroe, (MadHat Press, 2017).

TRANSLATION

The Collected Poems of Lucio Piccolo, with Ruth Feldman,
(Princeton University Press, 1972).
Selected Poetry of Andrea Zanzotto, with Feldman,
(Princeton University Press, 1976).
Shema: Collected Poems of Primo Levi, with Feldman,
(The Menard Press, 1975).
*Collected Poems of Primo Levi,*with Feldman,
(Faber and Faber, 1988).
The Dawn Is Always New: Selected Poems Of Rocco Scotellaro,
with Feldman, (Princeton University Press, 1979).
The Dry Air of the Fire: Selected Poems of Bartolo Cattafi, with Feldman,
(Ardis/ Translation Press, 1981).
Primele Poeme / First Poems of Tristan Tzara, with Michael Impey,
(New Rivers Press, 1976).
Selected Poems of Tudor Arghezi, with Impey,
(Princeton University Press, 1976).
Currents and Trends: Italian Poetry Today, edited, with many translations,
with Feldman, (New Rivers Press, 1979).
Euripides' *The Phoenician Women,* translated with Peter Burian,
(Oxford University Press, 1981).
The Hands of the South: Selected Poems of Vittorio Bodini, with Feldman,
(Charioteer Press, 1981).
Rain One Step Away: Selected Poems of Milih Cevdat Anday,
with Talat Halman, (Charioteer Press, 1981).
Rome, Danger to Pedestrians by Rafael Alberti,
(Quarterly Review of Literature Contemporary Poetry Series, 1984).
Garden of the Poor: Selected Poems of Rocco Scotellaro, with Feldman,
(Cross Cultural Communications, 1992).

CHILDREN

The Tongue Dancing, (Rowan Tree Press/ Simon and Schuster, 1984).
The Fox and the Buffalo, (Green Tiger Press, 1985).
A Basket Full of White Eggs, (Orchard Books / Franklin Watts, 1988).
Turtle and the Race Around the Lake, (Sierra Oaks Publishing, 1996).
The House With No Door: African Riddle-poems,
(Browndeer Press/Harcourt Brace, 1998).
Touching the Distance: Native American Riddle-poems,
(Browndeer Press/Harcourt Brace, 1998).

EDITING

Smoothing the Ground: Essays on Native American Oral Literature,
(University of California Press, 1982).
Recovering the Word: Essays on Native American Literature with Arnold Krupat,
(University of California Press, 1987).
I Tell You Now: Autobiographical Essays by Native American Writers,
with Krupat, (University of Nebraska Press, 1987).
Poetry From The Amicus Journal,
(Tioga Press, 1990).
On the Translation of Native American Literatures,
(Smithsonian Institution Press, 1992).
*Coming to Light: Contemporary Translations of the Native Literatures
of North America,* (Random House, 1995).
Native American Songs and Poems, An Anthology,
(Dover Publications, 1996).
Here First: Autobiographical Essays by Native American Writers, with Krupat,
(Modern Library, 2000).
Poetry Comes Up Where It Can: Poems from the Amicus Journal, 1990-2000,
(University of Utah Press, 2000).
*Voices From Four Directions: Contemporary Translations of the Native Literatures
of North America,* (University of Nebraska Press, 2004).
*Algonquian Spirit: Contemporary Translations of the Algonquian
Literatures of North America,* (University of Nebraska Press, 2005).
Born in the Blood: On Translating Native American Literature,
(University of Nebraska Press, 2011).
Sky Loom: Native American Myth, Story Song,
(University of Nebraska Press, 2014).